Longman Self-help guides

Parents' rights in education

Felicity Taylor

Longman

Longman Group UK Limited,
Longman House, Burnt Mill, Harlow,
Essex CM20 2JE, England
and Associated Companies throughout the world.

First published 1986

British Library Cataloguing in Publication Data

Taylor, Felicity
Parents' rights in education. — (Longman self-help guides)
1. Educational law and legislation — Great Britain — Handbooks, manuals, etc.
2. Parent and child (Law) — Great Britain — Handbooks, manuals etc.
I. Title
370.19'31 KD3600.Z9

ISBN 0-582-89323-2

Set in 10/12pt Linotron Plantin
Printed in Great Britain
by Mackays, Chatham, Kent

Foreword

The object of this handbook is to help parents understand how the education system works, so that they can support their children's schools and their children's education. Parents and schools must work together if children are to do well.

It also explains how parents can influence schools and bring about changes if these are needed. Each chapter takes a theme – choosing a school, the curriculum, parents in school, special needs, teachers and teaching, rules and discipline, health and safety, finance. It sets out the underlying principles and rules, and describes what happens in practice. The aim is to equip parents with the basic information they need to make their own decisions about what can or ought to be done. The last chapter explains how power is distributed among the schools, the local education authorities and the government. It gives some hints on how to complain and how to campaign.

Though this is a handbook of parents' rights, it would be a pity if schools took it in a negative way. I believe that what the great majority of parents want is for their children to do well and be happy at school. This is what schools want too. Any barriers between them owe more to poor communication and misunderstanding than to lack of goodwill on either side, or to any real conflict of interest. Parents who understand the system, and the difficulties schools face, can be a valuable source of support which our schools cannot afford to neglect or underestimate.

I would like to thank all the many parents, teachers, governors and officers I have met in the last 15 years. They have all helped me to write this book. One of the reasons why education gets such a hold over those of us involved in any way is that you are always learning something new and interesting, sometimes shocking, often encouraging, from the people you meet in schools. Very special thanks to Jenny Saxon who typed the script to a standard of perfection that put me to shame.

Felicity Taylor

About the author

Felicity Taylor has been a governor of primary, secondary, special and independent progressive schools, and is at present governor of an ILEA school for children with severe learning difficulties and on the management committee of Elfrida Rathbone, Camden. She has researched into vandalism in schools and accountability in education, and has been instrumental in several educational campaigns, the latest appointment being the National Chair of the National Association of Governors and Managers (1983–86). She has a degree from Oxford and a University of London Diploma, and is married with four children.

Contents

1

Your right to choose a school

Local education authorities, (LEAs), must make sure that there is enough suitable education for all the children in their area. Suitable is defined in the 1944 Act as 'sufficient in number, character, and equipment to afford for all pupils opportunities for education offering such variety of instruction and training as may be desirable in view of their different ages, abilities and aptitudes'. LEAs do not have to provide all the colleges and schools that are needed; they can use facilities provided by other LEAs, or by voluntary organisations, or even, in exceptional circumstances, by independent schools. But it is the LEA's duty to see that there is a suitable place for every child that wants one. Some parents may choose to pay for private education, others may want to educate their child at home, but all children have the right to a free place in a school that meets their needs. This applies to children with learning difficulties, however severe, just as much as to anyone else.

Parents also have a right to have their preferences about their children's education taken into account. The law is based on the important principle that children should be educated in accordance with their parents' wishes, unless there are overriding reasons against it. It is easy to overlook this when there are so many reasons why parents cannot always have the education they want for their child. Yet parents should never underestimate that fundamental right to have their views considered. Nor should teachers or education officers.

County and voluntary schools

Within the state system of education, there are two kinds of school 'maintained' out of public funds – *county schools* whose buildings, staff and resources are all provided by LEAs, and *voluntary schools*, which were originally set up by churches and charities. The staff and day-to-day running costs of all voluntary schools are paid by the LEA, but voluntary schools have to pay for their own buildings, repairs and alterations. (They receive an 85% grant from central government funds towards this.) There are three kinds of voluntary school: *aided* and *special agreement* schools have more independence from the LEA than *controlled* schools.

There is an important difference between county and voluntary schools as far as choosing a school is concerned. It is the LEA who decides how places should be allocated at all its county schools. Each voluntary school can make its own arrangements for admissions, though if it has made an agreement with the LEA about how places should be allocated, it must stick to this.

Parents need to remember this distinction when choosing a school, as it can affect their chances of getting a place at the school they want.

Pre-school education

LEA nursery schools and classes

LEAs no longer have to provide nursery education though most of them choose to do so. They may run nursery schools, or nursery classes attached to primary schools. These usually have a daily morning and an afternoon session, but many children attend only one of these. The terms are the same as other school terms.

The DES regulations state that the ratio of children to adults must be not more than 13.1 and there must be at least one qualified teacher for every 26 children. They also specify standards for space and facilities, including outside play space.

Normally you apply for a place to the headteacher of the nursery or primary school. They decide who gets places, though the LEA may give guidance about this. If places are in short supply, priority is given to children with special education needs, or social needs.

The provisions of the 1980 Act about choice of school do not apply to nursery schools, so there is no legal right of appeal if you cannot get the place you want. However, you could appeal to the local education officer in charge of nursery education, and then to the members of the Education Committee if you felt you had been turned down unfairly.

There is no charge for nursery education provided by your LEA in nursery schools or classes.

Pre-school playgroups

Playgroups may be run by a group of parents, or by a voluntary organisation. They have to be registered with the local Social Services Department, which lays down standards for the accommodation and may insist that at least some of the staff are qualified. Parents are usually expected to take an active part in the organisation and staffing of the group on a volunteer basis.

The organisers decide who should get places in a playgroup, but they are unlikely to turn anyone away if they have room. There may be a small fee per session, but this may be subsidised if parents cannot afford to pay.

There is plenty of help available if you want to start your own playgroup. Local councils may give grants, and the Pre-School Playgroups Association can give information, advice and training.

Independent nursery schools and playgroups

Private nursery schools and playgroups run on a commercial basis may be registered with and inspected by Social Services or they may be registered with the DES like other independent schools, and subject to the same regulations. You apply to the school for a place. Costs are similar to other private school fees.

Day nurseries

Although day nurseries traditionally concentrate on providing day care for the under-fives, rather than education, and are staffed by nursery nurses, the 1980 Education Act made it possible for LEAs to provide teachers to work part-time in day nurseries, together with the necessary equipment and resources.

In some areas, nursery centres have been set up, staffed by nursery nurses and teachers working together to provide full-time and part-time day care and pre-school education on a joint basis.

All day nursery provision is in short supply, and places are allocated by Social Services to families in the most need.

Local councils providing day nurseries can make a means-tested charge for the service, whether or not education is provided by the LEA.

Primary schools

The first stages of formal school can be organised in two ways:

Infant schools for children of 5–7, with
Junior schools for children of 7–11

often combined in one primary school under one head

or

First schools for children of 5–8/9, with
Middle schools for children of 8/9–12/13

Normally the heads of both county and voluntary primary schools arrange admissions to their school, though they must follow the published rules. So the first stage in getting a place is to go and see the head.

Secondary schools

The most common type of secondary school is the 'all-through' comprehensive for pupils of 11–18 years of age.

In some areas there are 11–16 schools and sixth-form colleges which provide sixth-form courses for a number of schools, or tertiary colleges which provide all kinds of courses, including technical and vocational studies, for people over 16.

Because there is often competition for places at popular secondary schools, admission to county schools may be handled at the Education Offices. Voluntary schools arrange their own admissions. This is usually done by the head. Sixth form and tertiary colleges also make their own arrangements in most cases.

You can get details of how admissions are organised from the local Education Office. (See **How to find out about schools**, page 12.)

Special schools

These are schools which cater for children with special educational needs, either with a particular kind of handicap, such as deafness, or with other learning difficulties. They are often all-age schools.

Non-maintained special schools

Non-maintained special schools are not maintained by the LEAs; they receive grants for buildings and maintenance direct from the DES. They are normally run by charities such as the Spastics Society, but most of the fees for children attending them are paid by LEAs because they provide specialised education not available in the LEAs' own schools.

Non-maintained special schools are subject to many of the same DES regulations as maintained schools, and must include elected parents and teachers on their governing body.

Sponsorship from an LEA is normally required to get a place.

Independent schools

The DES definition of an independent school is 'any fee-paying school of five or more pupils of compulsory school age'. Independent schools are not subject to the regulations laid down by the DES or LEAs for maintained schools, but they must apply for registration to the DES. They can be refused registration or struck off the register if the Secretary of State is satisfied that the premises, the head or the staff are unsuitable, or the education being provided is not appropriate for the pupils.

Independent schools are free to make their own choice of pupils. This is usually the responsibility of the head. Details about the procedure for admission will normally be published in the school prospectus. The Independent Schools Information Service (ISIS) publishes regional directories of independent schools.

Sometimes an LEA has an arrangement with an independent school to take up a number of its places each year. If so, the LEA must publish details giving the names of the schools, the number of places in each school, and the rules by which it allocates the places available.

See **Assisted places**, page 152 for details of help with independent education.

Education otherwise than at school

Some parents do not want their children to go to school at all. They prefer to educate them at home. Although this is an option permitted under the 1944 Act, parents face considerable difficulty if they choose it, unless they can afford full-time private tutors.

The Act says that parents have a duty to see that their children receive efficient full-time education suitable for their ages and aptitudes, either at school or otherwise. The LEA will require schedules of work, samples of written work, and other evidence of progress in a wide range of subjects. If the LEA is not satisfied, it may serve a school attendance order on the parent, and if the attendance order is ignored, the parents can be taken to court, and the child may be taken into care.

Education Otherwise is an association set up to advise and support parents who wish to educate their children at home.

Children with special needs

When in exceptional circumstances a child cannot go to school full-time, the LEA can make alternative arrangements, perhaps by providing individual tuition, or by allowing part-time education, for instance in a hospital school. (See pages 79–81)

Single sex and co-education

Almost all primary and middle schools are co-educational. In secondary schools the proportion of mixed to single sex schools is about 50%. However, the schools are not evenly distributed, and the demand for places does not always match the supply. There may be a surplus of single-sex places in some areas, not enough in others.

Although this is a subject about which many parents feel very strongly, the fact that you prefer single sex or co-education does not guarantee you a place in the 'right' kind of school. If there are not enough places to go round, your preference will be taken into account, but children living nearest to the school are likely to get priority.

Some parents want a girls' school for their daughters because of religious beliefs. However, the official view is that co-educational schools are able to make special arrangements for girls which allow for religious customs. Religious beliefs are not, therefore, an overriding reason for getting a place at a single sex school.

Under the terms of the Sex Discrimination Act 1975, it is illegal for a co-educational school to make any distinction on grounds of sex when allocating places, even if this results in the boys far outnumbering the girls in a school, or vice versa. At one time, a concession was made that the rules could be adjusted to prevent the proportion of one sex dropping below 40%, but this is now withdrawn. The rules about allocation must be applied in exactly the same way to each applicant, regardless of sex.

Single sex schools are, of course, exempt from this rule, and single sex schools becoming co-educational are allowed to make special arrangements during the changeover.

When must a child go to school?

The law lays down the ages between which a child must be receiving full-time education, ie the period when parents have a duty to see that their child is being educated, and when LEAs must make a suitable place available.

Starting school

Children must begin full-time education at the beginning of the term after their fifth birthday. So even if a child's birthday is only a few days after term starts the LEA does not have to provide a place until the next term. Many people feel that this puts children born in the summer months at a disadvantage. They may not start school until the autumn, and so have only two years in the infants, whereas children born earlier in the school year can get three years' infant schooling.

Nowadays, many LEAs offer autumn places to all their 'rising fives' – that is, children who will have their fifth birthday before the next autumn term – so that they all get three years in the infants. However, children with summer birthdays who are only just four may not be ready for full-time school. Younger children may be allowed to attend part-time, but parents cannot insist on this. The alternative is to decide to wait until the child is five before accepting a place.

Birth certificates

A birth certificate must usually be shown when a child starts school, so that the school has legal proof of the child's age. If parents refuse to produce this, the LEA can apply for a copy from the Registrar of Births and Deaths. Copies of birth certificates are obtainable for a fee of £1.50 from the Superintendent Registrar of the district where the child's birth was registered, or from the General Register Office, St Catherine's House, 10 Kingsway, London WC2B 6JP.

If parents cannot produce a birth certificate, perhaps because their child was not born in Great Britain, a sworn affidavit may be accepted instead. The onus is on the parents to prove the child's age, especially in any court proceedings about not attending school.

Leaving school

Pupils can leave school when they are sixteen, but only on two dates in the year. Those with birthdays between September 1 and January 31 may not leave before the end of the spring term. Those with birthdays between February 1 and August 31 can leave on the

Friday before the last Monday in May, that is at the summer half-term.

Choosing to stay on at school

If you wish to continue your education after the age of 16, the LEA has a duty to provide facilities in school or college for you to do so free of charge, up to the age of 19. This applies to students with special educational needs in the same way as to everyone else.

Many people who stay on for three years in the sixth form have their nineteenth birthday during the school year, but it would be unreasonable, in terms of the 1944 Act, for the LEA or the school to ask them to leave in mid-course because of their age.

Boarding education

Sometimes a child lives too far from the nearest suitable school to travel to and fro every day. The LEA must then provide a boarding school place or board and lodging near a suitable school, free of charge. The 1944 Act says that if boarding is necessary, parents' wishes about the religious affiliation of the person with whom the child is to board must be taken into account.

Under the 1944 Act, LEAs are also given the power to provide or pay towards the cost of boarding education for children who could attend a local day school, but whose parents would like them to go to a boarding school. Some LEAs run their own boarding schools, or boarding houses or hostels attached to day schools, some pay for children to attend another LEA's school, and others subsidise places at independent schools. However, there is no obligation on the LEA to offer any of these if the child could go to a local day school.

Common reasons for providing help with boarding are:

- The family has to move frequently because of a parent's job.
- Both parents are working abroad (not permanently) and the

schools there do not provide appropriate education.

- Difficult home circumstances, prejudicial to the child's welfare.
- Special educational needs because of learning difficulties or health problems.
- Exceptional talent that requires early training, eg, for dancing.

Each LEA has its own policy on providing boarding education and its own definition of need, and some are more generous than others. So it is important to get full details of the criteria used if you want to apply.

See **Fees**, pages 146 and 151, for more details of help with the cost of boarding.

School transport

The law recognises that children must be able to get to school if they are to be educated, and the 1944 Act makes it obligatory for LEAs to provide transport if children live more than walking distance from the nearest suitable school. (See **Grants**, page 145.)

However, if parents choose a school that is not the nearest one, there is no compulsion on the LEA to provide transport, though most LEAs will do this for parents who choose a denominational school. The law about providing transport was not changed in the 1980 Act, which gave parents more rights about choosing a school. Recognising that parents might not be able to afford to choose a school if the LEA would not give any help with travel costs, the DES issued a Circular Letter (15th December 1981) which asked LEAs to look sympathetically at the need to provide help with transport to parents who chose schools which were not the nearest to their home, especially in the case of voluntary schools serving a wide area.

LEAs were reminded that parents should be fully informed about the help offered with school transport before they made their choice of school.

How to find out about schools

Information from LEAs

It is not difficult for parents to get the basic information they need about schools, because the 1980 Act makes it compulsory for LEAs and school governors to publish this. The information must be freely available to parents and copies should be available for distribution in all local schools and education offices, and for reference in public libraries. Copies must go to all parents the year before their child is due to transfer to secondary school.

The information from LEAs must cover the following points:

- Addresses of local education offices.
- How parents can get information about individual schools.
- Names, addresses and telephone number of each school in the LEA area, with the expected number of pupils and their ages, type of school, and any religious affiliation.
- In Wales, the policy on Welsh teaching, generally and in each school.
- Arrangements for transfer to other schools, with details of the rules by which places are allocated.
- Provision of school transport.
- Policy on provision of milk and meals, how these are charged for and what help with the cost is available.
- Provision of school clothing, and uniform grants, giving the address where to apply for more information.

- Details of other grants and allowances and where to apply for these.
- General policy on entry for public exams.
- Policies for special educational needs and where parents can find out more about these.
- Any changes planned to begin after the start of the school year.

LEAs must also make information about special educational provision available on request to parents, and ensure that there are reference copies in education offices, schools and libraries.

This must cover:

- Detailed arrangements and policies on identification and assessment.
- Provision for children with special needs in county, voluntary and maintained special schools.
- The use made of places in non-maintained special schools and independent schools.
- How parents can obtain help and information.
- Transport arrangements.
- Where to find out more about individual schools.
- Any changes planned to begin after the start of the school year.

Information from individual schools

The LEA, or the governors of an aided school, must also arrange for the publication, in the same way, of information about individual schools. This must cover:

- The name, address and telephone number, and the type of school.
- The name of the head and of the chair of governors.
- Specific arrangements for parents to visit the school if they are considering it for their child.

- Details of the school curriculum, including the curriculum for different ages, the arrangements for choosing subjects, the policy on sex education.
- For secondary schools, the level up to which different subjects are taught.
- Any religious affiliation.
- Details of religious education and the arrangements for parents to ask for their children to be excused religious instruction.
- Arrangements for children with special educational needs.
- In Wales, the policy on Welsh teaching.
- How children are grouped for teaching and the policy on homework.
- Arrangements for pastoral care – care for the children's welfare.
- Arrangements for discipline, including the use of corporal punishment and how parents and pupils are informed about school rules.
- Policy on school uniform and the cost of this.
- School clubs and societies and other activities.
- Careers advice in schools with pupils of secondary age.
- Any changes planned to begin after the start of the school year.
- For schools with pupils over 15, except special schools, details about entry to public exams, the age at which these are taken, the total number of pupils in that year, the number of pupils in the year group taking GCE and CSE exams and the grades they obtained.

School prospectus

Many schools publish their own prospectus, which includes all the legally required information together with a fuller description of the school and its work. The contents can be very informative, and the way the information is presented can also tell you something about the character of the school. Is it friendly and welcoming? Does it use pupil's work as illustration? Or is the language rather formal and off-putting?

Local reputation

More people probably choose a school from its local reputation than from any other information. Yet the reputation a school has may not bear much relation to what goes on inside the school. So it is important to cross-check what you hear about a school in the local shops and community centres. Listen to what parents whose children are still at the school (and preferably the pupils themselves) have to say before you make up your mind. Ask if you can talk to the parent governors, or pupils at the top of the school. If the answer is no, you may well wonder why.

Visiting the school

You should never choose a school without going to see it first. A good school will make this easy, although at busy times of the year they may prefer to arrange special open days for prospective parents rather than encourage individual visits.

When you have read the published information, make a checklist of the points you think most important along with a note of any questions you want to ask. This helps to make the visit more rewarding, and also makes it easier to compare one school with another.

See as many schools as possible, even if you are not considering some of them. The more you see, the better you get at making a judgement, as it becomes less daunting, and easier to assess the atmosphere. It may be a good plan not to visit your favoured school first, as if you have seen other schools, you have a better standard of comparison.

There is something about the atmosphere of a good school that is easy to recognise, difficult to describe – busy without being disorganised, lively but not noisy, friendly and welcoming to visitors. Clear sign-posting, children's recent work on display, staff who know most of the pupils (and their colleagues) by name, how people speak to one another; these are all indications of morale, which add an extra dimension to the factual information about courses and exams.

Making the final choice

Though there are plenty of sources of information and advice, choosing a school is a very personal business, and in the end, you know what seems right for you and your family. No school will be perfect, or offer everything you want, so you have to weigh up which factors matter most to you.

When you are thinking of choosing a popular school, it is essential to find out how the places are allocated, (see below), and what your chances of getting one are likely to be. If they are not good, you have to decide whether it is worth the risk of disappointment. You have to take into account whether you might be missing a better chance of a place at your second choice. That may also be a popular school and likely to fill up at the first choice stage. The head and the education officer in charge of allocations should be able to advise you about this.

At least, when you have all the relevant facts, you can make an informed decision; you won't think, afterwards, 'If only I'd known . . .'.

How places are allocated

It is up to the LEA or the governors of a voluntary aided school to decide the rules for getting places at a particular school. They have to take parents' preferences into account, but these can be over-ruled. The three reasons which the law allows for not complying with parents' wishes are:

- It would prejudice the provision of efficient education or the efficient use of resources. (In other words, the school is full, and there are empty places at other schools.)
- It would be incompatible with the arrangements agreed by the LEA with an aided school about admissions to that school. (For example, a Roman Catholic school may give priority to Catholic children.)
- The school is a selective school and the child is refused admission on the basis of ability or aptitude.

When is a school full?

The LEA or the governors must publish the number of places available at each school. This may be less than the number for which the school was built. Because of the steady fall in the birthrate many LEAs have reduced the size of schools as an alternative to closing some schools altogether.

Once the stated number of places at a school has been allocated, the school can refuse to take any more pupils. However, a court case in South Glamorgan set an important precedent. The court said that the LEA could not use the fact that the allotted number of places had already been filled as the reason for turning down a child, because the LEA had already breached the limit by allowing other extra children into the school in question. It could not, therefore, automatically prove that allowing this extra pupil in would damage the education provided in the school. This led to the statement of principle that when damage might be caused to the education provided in a school by admitting another pupil, the potential damage has to be weighed against the strength of the case put forward by the parent.

Religion and choice

Church schools often serve a wider area than local county schools. If they give priority to church members, they should explain what evidence of belonging to the church is required. It is not usually good enough to claim nominal membership; you may have to show that you attend church regularly, and support church activities.

Some schools will also give preference to practising members of other faiths, especially if they have no local church school.

Many diocesan authorities urge church schools, especially Church of England schools which represent the Established Church, to take into account their responsibility to the community as a whole, and accept children who though not from religious families, may benefit from the kind of education a church school provides. These 'compassionate' reasons for taking children are difficult to define. The head will normally interview the parents and the child, and decide on that basis.

Selection by ability

Where selective schools still exist, the LEA or the governors must publish details of how the selection is made. If parents feel that their child has been unfairly rejected, they will have to produce substantial evidence to support their case. This might be reports from the child's present school, from an educational psychologist, preferably one employed by the LEA, or medical or other evidence to show that there was some good reason why a child performed badly in a particular test or on a particular day.

Some LEAs assess a child's ability in order to obtain a 'balance of ability' in comprehensive schools. The aim is to prevent some schools taking too many children assessed as top ability, or low ability. They will have to publish details of how many places in each ability band are expected to be available at each school. They may then refuse children places because their particular band is full, though there may be vacancies in other bands.

Race discrimination

It is illegal for any school to discriminate against anyone on grounds of race, when deciding which children should be admitted to a school. Discrimination means treating them less favourably because of their ethnic group. The head of an independent school was prosecuted under the Race Relations Act 1976 because he refused to admit a Sikh boy unless he cut his hair and ceased to wear a turban. His reason was that these customs would emphasise racial differences among the pupils. The court ruled that no discrimination occurred because the Sikhs belonged to a social group, not a racial group. The boy's parents appealed to the House of Lords, who ruled in his favour on three grounds:

Firstly, the definition of a racial or ethnic group meant a group of people with a shared history, who regarded themselves as a group, and who were regarded as a group by others. Other relevant characteristics of an ethnic group were a common geographical origin or common ancestors, a common language and heritage, a common religion, and being members of an oppressed minority or a dominant group. So although their physical and racial characteristics were no different from other people who lived in the Punjab, the Sikhs were a clearly defined ethnic group because of these factors.

Secondly, though Sikhs could comply in physical terms with the requirement to cut their hair and not wear a turban, their cultural heritage forbade it, and the boy could not remain a Sikh without long hair and a turban.

Thirdly, the fact that the head believed that the school would provide better education if it was allowed to discriminate against people wearing turbans was not justifiable within the meaning of the Act.

What happens when a school is over-subscribed?

The LEA or the governors must publish details of the rules by which the allocation is made when there are more applicants than places. They must list the criteria they use, and their order of priority. The criteria usually include:

- The nearness of the school to the home. (Some authorities take travel facilities into account, others measure on a map as the crow flies, others draw a catchment area or zone around each of their schools.)
- Having a brother or sister or other family connection with the school.
- Special medical or social reasons.

For voluntary schools:

- Parents being practising members of the church.
- Children having been christened or otherwise formally enrolled in the church.

It is important to read the criteria carefully, as they vary considerably, particularly for the voluntary schools. Always mention any special reasons or connection with the school when you first apply for a place, and produce supporting evidence, for example, a doctor's letter if you are claiming medical reasons. It may be too late afterwards. The rules are then used to decide who should get places. So if living in the school's catchment area is the first criterion, all the children in that area who have applied for the school are given places first. If there are any places left, and the next criterion is having a brother or sister already in the school, these children will get places, though they do not live in the catchment area. And so on.

Stages in choosing a school

- Write or telephone the Education Offices – address in the telephone book or library – and ask for information about the local school system.
- When you receive this, make a list of suitable local schools within reach of your home.
- Ask them for their prospectus and details of how to visit.
- Gather all the information you can and draw up a short-list of schools.
- Visit these schools.
- List pros and cons of each school, including your chances of getting a place, and make your choice.

What to do if you are refused a place in the school you choose

Parents must be given a chance to discuss their choice with the LEA. If they cannot reach agreement, the parents have a formal right of appeal to an independent Appeals Committee.

Appeals Committees

The LEA must set up a panel of members to serve on Appeals Committees for county schools. Voluntary school governors must set up a panel, to which the LEA also nominates members, for their school.

The panels consist of local people with an interest in education. Representatives of the LEA or the governors on any Committee must not outnumber the other members by more than one. Members of the LEA or governors of the school may not take the chair, and the clerk must not be otherwise involved in the appeals procedure. None of the committee members must have any previous connection with the cases to be heard. The procedure follows a Code of Practice drawn up by the Council on Tribunals. Full notice of how to appeal, any time limit, and details of the procedure must be given to parents in writing. Parents should get proper notice of the date of the hearing, and a week beforehand they should be sent details of the reasons why they were not given the chosen place.

When parents are presenting their case to the Appeals Committee, it is important to state it very fully. It is easy to miss out important information, perhaps because it seems too obvious to mention. This is where a friend may be able to give advice and support.

The Code of Practice recommends that the hearing should be conducted as informally as possible. Parents may bring a friend, who speaks for them if necessary. Interpreters should be provided for parents whose first language is not English.

The parents and the LEA or governors are asked to state their case, and can ask questions about each other's evidence. Members of the committee can also ask questions.

How the decision is taken

The Committee must first decide if the LEA or the governors have followed their own published rules about the allocation of places. If not, they decide in favour of the parent.

If the rules were followed correctly, the Committee then has to consider whether, if the child was admitted to the school, education would be prejudiced. The LEA or the governors will probably claim that the school is full, that there is no more room in the classroom, that teachers may refuse to teach classes with more than a certain number of pupils, that resources have been provided for a fixed number of pupils, and that spare capacity is available in another school which will be wasted if it is not taken up. If the Committee decide that education would not be prejudiced, they rule in favour of the parent.

If the Committee think that it could be prejudiced, they then have to weigh up the parents' reasons for wanting that particular place, against the damage that might be done to the school by taking an extra child. They take their decision according to the individual circumstances of that case.

So even if the LEA or the governors have acted correctly throughout, they can still be over-ruled.

Appeals Committees seem to look favourably on appeals based on the social needs of the child, or where the system appears to work against natural justice in that particular case.

The decision of the Appeals Committee is binding on the LEA or the governors.

Further appeals

Parents who are turned down can pursue their appeal. They can appeal to the Secretary of State under section 68 of the 1944 Act, on the grounds that the Appeals Committee have acted unreasonably in rejecting their appeal.

If the parents think that maladministration has taken place in the way places were allocated, they can appeal to the local Ombudsman. Parents can also apply to the High Court for a judicial review of the way the tribunal heard their case, if they feel that an important point of law is involved.

It has to be said that very few of these further appeals are successful.

Waiting lists

Some LEAs and voluntary aided schools keep a waiting list of disappointed applicants. Since the turnover of pupils is fairly high, especially in urban areas, people near the top of the list may stand a good chance of getting a place within a few months. But there is a difficulty if people who make a formal appeal are given places, perhaps over the heads of people on the waiting list. If you are told that you can go on the waiting list, you should check with the school whether it is also advisable to make a formal appeal.

Some primary schools keep an informal waiting list of under-fives in their district, who will want to come to the school when they are old enough. Unless you have a formal letter offering you a place, there may be no guarantee of getting one just because you put your name down. So check with the school what the arrangements are.

Keeping your child out of school

Some parents keep their children out of school altogether until they get a place at their chosen school. There is no longer any legal advantage in doing this since the rules about attendance orders were changed. The question is will the authority give priority as a result of this pressure, or will it take the parents to court for failing to send their child to school? You do need to think very carefully about whether being at the centre of this kind of row is likely to do more harm to a child's education than attending a different school, even if it is not the one you prefer.

Stages in making an appeal

- When your child is refused a place, ask for an interview with the education officer responsible, to discuss the alternatives.
- If you cannot reach agreement, write a formal letter of appeal – the LEA or the school may have a special form for this – setting out fully all the reasons why you want that school.
- The LEA or the school will send you the reasons why you were not given a place.
- An Appeals Committee will hear your case and that of the authority or school and will decide.
- If they support you, you will get the place you want.

- If they turn you down, you can consider:

  an appeal to the Secretary of State, if you think their decision is unreasonable in law;

  a complaint to the Ombudsman if the procedure has not been carried out properly;

  an appeal to the High Court if a point of law is involved;

  or

  accepting a place in another school and making the best of it.

2 What rights do you have over how and what your child learns?

Issues about how a school is organised, and what is taught are often of great significance yet parents have very little direct influence over them. Proposals in the White paper *Better schools* would increase their influence to some extent. In the Education Bill, published February 1986, which is based on the White paper, it is suggested that every school would call an annual meeting at which parents could discuss a report on the year's activities prepared by the school and the governing body. When at least 10% of parents were present,
voting could take place on formal resolutions about the contents of the report, which the governors and the school would have to consider and report back on. What practical difference this would make to the running of the school remains to be seen, but it would enable parents to make their views known.

School organisation

In spite of all the educational changes that have taken place in the last twenty years, the basic unit of school organisation is still the class in the classroom, a group of pupils working with a teacher. The head has the right to decide how the school should be organised, which children should be in which class and who should teach them. There are a variety of ways of deciding how schools should be organised, and parents have very little influence on any of them. These decisions are firmly in the hands of the head and staff.

STREAMING

Streaming is a method of dividing children according to their attainments into a number of groups or streams which remain the same for all lessons. The higher streams may be groomed for public exams; lower streams can easily lose confidence in their own abilities. Once children have been placed in a particular stream, it is rare for transfers to take place, though the school may deny this.

BANDING

Banding is a way of grouping children into broader bands of ability for all lessons, with perhaps several parallel classes in each band in each year.

SETTING

Setting is the most common form of grouping in secondary schools. Pupils are grouped according to their abilities in different subjects, so that someone might be in the top set for Maths, the second set for English and the third set for History.

MIXED ABILITY GROUPING

Mixed ability grouping does not use attainment as the basis for organising children in classes, so each class covers a wide range of ability. Those who prefer it say that it gives all children the opportunity to develop at their own pace. Most primary schools operate on a mixed ability basis, and many secondary schools use it especially in the lower part of the school.

If you feel that your child has been placed in the wrong band or set, you can make representations to the school. You will need to produce some supporting evidence, perhaps from a previous school or teacher. You cannot insist on a change.

Primary schools

Primary school children spend most of the day with the same class teacher especially in the younger age groups. Sometimes two or three classes work together with several teachers; this is known as team-teaching. As the children move up the school they may swop teachers for some lessons, so that, for example, the science specialist can give them regular science lessons.

Family grouping (or vertical grouping) is used in some primary schools. Instead of a class of seven year olds, one of eight year olds and so on, there might be two parallel classes with children of 7–9, and two for children of 9–11. This has the advantage of allowing children to progress naturally through the stages of learning without changing classes, so that the quick learners are not held back because of their age, and the slower developers are not moved up a class before they are ready.

The relationship between a primary school child and the class teacher can influence the child's educational and social progress very considerably. It may be difficult to change teachers when a child is unhappy (especially if there is only one class for each age group). This may not matter so much if the class teacher changes each year, but some schools have a system in which the teacher moves up with the class, so that the group has the same teacher throughout their infant or junior school career.

Parents can ask the head if their child can change classes, but heads are often reluctant to agree, particularly if one teacher is generally unpopular with parents. If the problem is long-term and serious, the only solution may be to change schools.

Secondary schools

In whatever way the school arranges its teaching groups for different subjects, each secondary school has some form of tutorial system to look after the pupils' welfare – or pastoral care as the jargon has it. This is normally based on tutor groups which may be horizontal or vertical – the group may all be the same age, or it may consist of pupils from each year group in the school. Most teachers in the school who do not have senior responsibilities will be class tutors. They may stay with the same tutor group throughout the school, or may change groups every year.

House and year systems are a way of dividing up large schools into more manageable units. Again, they may be divided horizontally, into year groups, with perhaps an Upper, Middle and Lower School, or vertically, into 'houses' covering the whole age range. Out-of-school activities, sports and social functions may be organised for houses and year groups, and they will normally have their own assembly and common room.

Schools vary in the importance they attach to tutor groups. If all the tutors have to do is call the register in the morning and afternoon, and there is no space on the timetable for tutor group activities, the system has very little value. If it is functioning well, you would normally go to the tutor first with any worry. So if your child had a social or welfare problem, you would go to the tutor, who might consult the education welfare officer or the head of house or year. If the problem was to do with a particular subject, the tutor should be able to put you in touch with the appropriate subject teacher or head of department. This should all be explained in the school brochure (see page 14).

The head carries the ultimate responsibility for school organisation, so if you cannot get satisfaction from the staff, or if you think your child would benefit from a change of tutor group, you go to the top. If the head cannot or will not help you, there is very little you can do. You can make an approach to the governors if you are seriously concerned about some aspect of the school's organisation but they will be reluctant to interfere on an internal matter. You will need to be able to show that a large number of other parents are also worried.

The school curriculum

What children learn in school and what they ought to learn have never been more controversial topics. Teachers prefer to regard this as a wholly professional matter; parents, governors, employers and Secretaries of State take a different view.

The Taylor Committee on school government considered that the curriculum comprised 'the sum of the experiences to which a child was exposed in school'. It was not a set of syllabuses and schemes of work that could be considered in isolation. The committee's description of how the curriculum should be planned and developed has generally been accepted. They identified four stages:

- Establishing the school's aims.
- Translating the aims into more specific goals; organising the school and developing teaching methods and other practical steps to achieve these goals.
- Keeping the education provided under continuous review and making regular appraisals of the school's progress.
- Deciding on action, to further the school's progress, and taking it.

How does this work in practice?

The head and staff in the nature of things, do most of the work of planning, organising and teaching – the nitty-gritty of timetabling, allocating time to different subjects, teaching methods, learning about new developments and putting them into practice. This is, after all, what they are paid for. But they do not have a free hand. Parents, local employers and the community have expectations about what schools should be doing that it is difficult to ignore, and there are professional constraints as well.

The public examination system, and the entrance requirements for higher education although they may be irrelevant to the needs of many pupils, exert the greatest pressure on the curriculum of the final years at secondary school. No school can escape entirely from being judged by its exam results.

The inspectorate, both local and national (see page 162) who monitor and assess what goes on in schools, advise on what should be taught, as well as on how it is taught. Local inspectors or advisers will want to make sure that schools carry out any LEA policies on the curriculum, for example on equal opportunities.

The DES, under Sir Keith Joseph, has taken a much more active role in attempting to influence the school curriculum. A series of curriculum policy statements have been issued, together with discussion documents from Her Majesty's Inspectorate (HMI). The aim is, according to the 1985 White paper *Better schools*, to reach 'a broad agreement about the objectives and content of the school curriculum', as part of the drive to raise educational standards. These publications have been received with varying degrees of enthusiasm by the teaching profession, who are opposed to central control over what is taught in schools. Direct intervention has also been tried. The government wants schools to be more aware of the world of work, so it set up the TVEI (Technical and Vocational Education Initiative). This is a five-year pilot programme with very generous funding from the Manpower Services Commission, which offers four-year courses for 14–19 year-olds leading to technical and vocational qualifications. It has proved very popular in some schools.

The governing body, which represents the community's interest in the school, is given the formal responsibility for overseeing its conduct and curriculum. The 1986 Education Bill promises an extension of that responsibility. In the past, it has indeed been a formality, but governing bodies were already taking it more seriously. It is now generally accepted that the head and staff should consult the governors about the school's aims, and are accountable to them for the way in which the school functions. Any new proposals or changes should be reported to the governors for discussion, and the governors are charged with keeping the school's performance under review. Through parent representation on the governing body, parents have a direct voice in how the curriculum develops, and can make their views known.

Equal opportunities and the curriculum

A good school will want to provide equal opportunities for all its pupils, will accept that very few people, including teachers, are completely free from prejudice, and will do its best to combat this by enlisting the help of governors, staff, parents and pupils. Without the support and commitment of all these groups, anti-racist and anti-sexist policies can do more harm than good.

SEX DISCRIMINATION

The Sex Discrimination Act 1975 makes any form of discrimination in education and training illegal. This means that it is against the law to treat any girl less favourably than a boy would be treated as regards 'the benefits, facilities and services' provided by the school. Boys must not be selected or tested on a different basis from girls.

In 1984, three girls won a case on these grounds against Bromley LEA and their school. Parents were told that the fourth year class was too big, so the youngest pupils would be kept down for a year, though they would do fourth year work. Eight girls were affected, and the parents of three of them claimed that discrimination had taken place because no boys were kept down. They asked for compensation for loss of status with their contemporaries, and damage said to have been done to their 11+ chances. The court awarded them £350 each.

Schools may not offer one course or subject only to boys and another only to girls, nor must they arrange the curriculum or timetable in such a way that it is difficult for boys or girls to follow particular courses. This does not mean that it is always wrong to provide separate classes for boys and for girls. This is allowed, in PE for example, as long as the facilities are equally good for both sexes.

Although this is now generally understood, and very few schools would deliberately break the law, unconscious prejudice about what is suitable for boys or girls still persists. The Equal Opportunities Commission published a leaflet *Do you provide equal opportunities?* which includes a useful set of questions any school might ask itself.

- Do boys and girls line up separately to move about the school?
- Are girls more often given the unexciting, monotonous tasks requiring more patience and concentration?
- Are boys more often given the unattrative, heavy, messy jobs requiring little or no sensitivity?
- Do boys always carry the milk crates?
- Do girls always put out the paints, etc?
- Are girls ever encouraged to operate the school's audio-visual or other mechanical aids?
- In thematic work, do girls always investigate clothes, food, home life, etc, while the boys research into weapons, building techniques, space travel, engines, etc?
- Is cookery restricted to girls and woodwork to boys?
- Are boys and girls segregated in classroom and assembly seating arrangements?
- Do boys and girls use separate playgrounds?
- Do you invite workpeople in non-traditional jobs to talk to pupils (e.g. female bus driver, male nurse, etc.)?
- Are girls and boys treated the same? Care should be taken not to react like the teacher who told a boy who could not knock a nail in to 'get on with it', but responds to a girl in the same situation by taking the wood, nail and hammer and doing it for her!
- Do the boys usually cover areas such as traffic surveys while the girls always do the work connected with plants, trees and pets?
- Are out-of-school activities so organised that the football club and the recorder club meet at the same time, thus becoming mutually exclusive?

There is plenty of evidence that discrimination still exists in some subjects. Girls are very under-represented in scientific and technical courses, boys in languages and home economics. It is easy for boys to monopolise computer equipment so that girls are excluded. Schools ought to do more to give positive encouragement to girls to take exam courses in science and maths, as these are essential qualifications for better jobs in a high technology future.

Some schools have found that organising girls-only classes in Maths and Computer Science in the early stages, helps girls to get over any diffidence they may feel at first.

Boys too need to be encouraged not to drop subjects like modern languages early on as this can limit their choice of career. It does boys no service if they are allowed to regard subjects like child development, home economics, as being only for girls. They need encouragement to take non-traditional options, which need presenting in a way that makes them seem relevant and interesting.

RACE DISCRIMINATION

The Race Relations Act (1976) makes it illegal for any educational establishments to discriminate against anyone on racial grounds, in the provision of its benefits, facilities or services. In other words, schools must not put any pupil at a disadvantage because of their racial origin. Very few schools would deliberately treat pupils less favourably because of their colour or nationality, but many do so by default, particularly as regards pupils whose first language is not English. There is also serious cause for concern about under-achievement of some black pupils, and the fact that some ethnic groups are over-represented in special schools.

The Swann Report on education of minority groups produced a mass of evidence on this topic, but was forced to the conclusion that there was no one single explanation or answer. The Report recommends that teaching English to those for whom it is not a first language should be carried out in the ordinary classroom, not in segregated centres or classes, because this causes unintentional discrimination.

Mother-tongue teaching is another controversial issue. This means giving children from minority groups instruction in their own language. An EEC directive issued in 1977 said that member states must promote the teaching of the mother-tongue and culture of minority groups in co-ordination with normal education. A DES Circular (No 5/81) interpreted this as meaning that LEAs should 'explore ways in which mother-tongue teaching might be provided, whether during or outside school hours, but not that they are required to give such tuition as of right'. Swann thought there were three questions: should children be taught in their own language, as in some Welsh schools; should children be encouraged to keep up their own language; and should these languages be taught like other modern languages, such as Spanish and Russian. Broadly speaking, the Swann Committee thought that the disadvantages of bi-lingual teaching outweighed the advantages, except as an aid to helping children in primary school whose first language was not English. It was the responsibility of the minority groups to preserve their own culture, language and traditions, though the LEA should foster this by providing facilities where necessary. There was a place for community languages in the ordinary modern language curriculum particularly where there was a significant number of children speaking that language in the school.

The report found that many schools had very little idea about what was meant by multi-cultural education, or understood the need for all schools, whether or not they had pupils from minority groups, to reflect the plural society in which all pupils will be living.

The title of the Swann Report is *Education for all.* Ann Dummett, Director of the Runnymede Trust, put her finger on what equal opportunities in education is really about. Writing in the magazine *Education* (22.3.85), she pointed out that a school which offers a false picture of the world to pupils is failing in its duty. 'Education for all should start by asking what we mean by "a good education" for any child, and should then work out by what means this good education can be provided for individual children in our very varied, unequal, regionally differentiated and thoroughly mixed school public.'

Religious education

Religious education is the one subject that has to be on every maintained school curriculum by law, though you might have to look rather hard in some schools to find it.

A compromise was worked out in the 1944 Act with the religious bodies who ran many existing schools. This made it compulsory for every maintained school to start the day with a corporate act of worship and teach some form of religious instruction. Voluntary aided and special agreement church schools can provide this instruction according to their own beliefs.

County schools must teach according to an agreed syllabus which is drawn up by a conference representing local churches. Voluntary controlled schools must teach to the agreed syllabus, but can also offer religious instruction according to their original trust deed if enough parents request it.

In the past the members of conferences preparing the agreed syllabus were mainly Christians, but there is no reason why other religions should not be represented. This is up to the LEA. The Inner London Education Authority recently drew up a new syllabus in which, according to the Church of England representative, 'Christianity features clearly but the syllabus honours the important place which other faiths have in contemporary London'. It includes discussion of Buddhism, Christianity, Hinduism, Islam, Judaism and Sikhism.

Parents who do not want their children to receive any religious instruction or to attend acts of worship can ask for their children to be withdrawn from these. The request has to come from the parent; the child is not allowed to express an opinion. If parents want a different kind of religious teaching, and there is no other school providing it which the child might reasonably attend, pupils may be excused school to attend religious instruction as long as it does not interfere with their other education. If a group of parents who want a special kind of religious teaching can supply a teacher at a suitable time, and there is no other way of providing it, the LEA must make suitable facilities available in the school.

Many schools now find it hard to hold an assembly for the whole school every day, and this requirement is not insisted on. Religious instruction may often be incorporated into a general syllabus dealing with moral and social issues. This can make it difficult for parents to know when to ask for their child to be withdrawn.

The right to opt out protects the freedom of the individual in a state system of education, but, in practice, the element of religious doctrine in what is taught in most schools is not offensive enough to make people of different beliefs (or none) feel strongly about it.

There are practical problems, such as the possibility of missing important notices if a child is not in assembly, or the need to supervise large numbers of children not attending Religious Education (RE). The issue may seem more acute where parents have to attend a church school because no other school is within easy reach. Schools ought in any case to ensure that proper arrangements are made for children who are withdrawn from RE and that they are not made to feel uncomfortable. This is something that parents can take up with the governors, if necessary.

Where religious beliefs are strongly felt, especially by parents belonging to non-Christian faiths, this has led to a demand for new voluntary schools for their children. The Swann Committee thought that this was unhelpful, mainly because such schools would be isolated from the mainstream of education. The Committee felt that a better solution was for schools to pay more attention to minority religious beliefs and customs, and to adopt a multi-faith approach. Proposals to set up a new voluntary school have to be published locally, so that local people who will be affected can object. Proposals have to be approved by the Secretary of State.

TEACHERS OF RELIGIOUS EDUCATION

Teachers in voluntary controlled and special agreement schools who are employed to give instruction according to the religious beliefs of the founding church are called 'reserved teachers', and can be dismissed for religious reasons. Non-reserved teachers cannot be required to teach RE. In voluntary controlled schools reserved teachers may not make up more than one in five of the staff and the head may not be a reserved teacher. In voluntary aided schools, the governors can make stipulations about religious education and beliefs for any teacher. Otherwise, no teacher must be at a disadvantage because of religious beliefs, refusal to teach RE, or attend church.

Physical education

It is one of the failures of our education system that so many pupils end up disliking PE and games. Every child ought to leave school with some capacity to enjoy physical activity, and an understanding of why health and fitness are worth having. *The curriculum from 5–16* suggests that schools should provide for three main strands of physical education:

- control, co-ordination and mobility through PE and dance;
- physical skills requiring the co-ordination of physical and mental faculties, like painting, shaping and cutting, playing musical instruments;
- an understanding of how the body works.

You may feel that this is a long way from what your child receives in the way of physical education, but at least it gives some idea of what should be offered. Many schools have developed a wider range of activities and sports.

PE and games which form part of the school curriculum are just as compulsory as any other timetabled subject. Schools will often accept a parent's note as a temporary excuse for a child not doing PE or games, but if there are long-term medical problems you will need to provide a doctor's certificate, and to make sure that the PE staff teaching your child are aware of the condition.

LEAs have a duty under the 1944 Act 'to secure that the facilities for primary, secondary and further education provided for their area include adequate facilities for recreation and social and physical training'. The *Standards for school premises regulations 1981* do not lay down what indoor PE facilities should be provided, except that in new buildings changing rooms should be available for all children over eight years old. Otherwise the regulations simply include PE facilities in the overall space allowances, which depend on the ages of the pupils in the school. There are requirements about outdoor pitches and playing fields, depending on the age and number of pupils.

PE CLOTHING

Heads can insist that special clothing is worn for games and PE, even when there is no other school uniform, especially if safety is involved. The LEA can help with the provision of games kit (see **Grants**, page 142) but is not obliged to do so. If there is a problem about the cost of games kit, this is something the parents' association might tackle, perhaps by raising funds for a communal supply, or making representations to the school about the need for a less expensive specification.

Political education

It is up to the head to decide whether political education should form part of the school curriculum. However, both the DES and HM Inspectorate, in various curriculum documents, have suggested that secondary schools ought to prepare their pupils to take part in political life, and therefore they need to be aware of the main political issues and what the political parties stand for. 'Political education (is) important if pupils are to understand the forces, issues and processes at work in society.' (*The curriculum from 5–16* HMI, 1985)

These ideas must be presented without bias. As long as opposing views are put forward in a fair and balanced way, suitable to the level of maturity of the pupils, there is no reason why controversial subjects should not be tackled. This applies too to the vexed question of 'Peace studies'. The White paper *Better schools* comes out against this as a separate subject, but many schools and colleges teach it, for example, the well-known independent international school Atlantic College. There are also proposals for a 'Peace studies' A level. The British Atlantic Committee, a pro-Nato organisation, has published a Peace studies syllabus, which is claimed to be impartial and non-controversial.

If parents are worried about the way political education is being taught, or not taught, in their child's school, they should ask to discuss it with the school, who should be prepared to produce detailed syllabuses and schemes of work. It is prudent to check that you have the facts right about the course and are not relying on hearsay if you intend to make a complaint. You can also approach the governors, and if you are not satisfied, the LEA.

Sir Keith Joseph, as Secretary of State, has reaffirmed that DES regulations about the style and content of political education are not necessary. It was for the school to decide, taking into account the views of parents. He did suggest that parents who could not get a response that satisfied them from the school or the LEA should make representations to the DES.

Sex education

The 1980 Act made it obligatory for schools to publish details about 'the manner and context in which education as regards sexual matters is given'. So parents now have the right to know how sex education is provided in a school. Very often this is in the context of health education, along with other contentious issues, like alcohol, drugs and smoking. Parents have a right to expect that the school's policy on health education will be well-informed, likely to do more good than harm, and not excessively alarmist. The DES has recently issued a free pamphlet, *Drug misuse and the young*, which has a useful list of organisations which can give expert advice and information on various aspects of health education.

It has always been held in the past that parents have no direct right to a say in how and what is taught in health education lessons, though most schools would pay attention to parents' views, and would allow them to withdraw their children from sex education if they felt very strongly about it. As with political education, the school has to be seen to be acting reasonably in the eyes of most parents. Most parents are happy for the school to given unbiassed information on these topics.

However, the Gillick case throws this interpretation of the law into disarray. It was suggested that even to give information about sex and contraception to pupils under 16 without their parents' consent would be illegal. The case was lost. Otherwise schools might have to get consent from each parent before giving any sex education.

Schools which take parents into their confidence and discuss their policy on health education, explaining the syllabus and how it is taught, normally have no difficulty in obtaining the approval of the majority of parents. If you feel that the policy is going astray, especially if other parents are also worried, you can take it up with the school and with the governing body.

Homework

Two hours' homework every night adds about half as much again to the school day, so it is not surprising that schools and parents think it is important. It can reinforce what children have been taught in school, and can help them to learn to work on their own. It can also use up a good deal of the children's free time, and prevent them from taking part in other worthwhile activities out of school. So can schools force children to do school work out of school hours? The answer is in theory no, in practice, yes.

Schools can make it one of the school rules that children have a reasonable amount of homework each week, and can also refuse to allow children who do not do homework to sit for important exams.

The amount of homework set, and how seriously it is taken, varies from school to school. Some set too much, some set too little and some do not bother about whether it is done or not. A good school will have a sensible homework policy about how much homework children of different ages should be given, and how the work is set and marked. It will have a system for checking up on whether the work is being done, and making sure that staff are marking and returning work regularly. The policy will have been discussed with parents, who will be told what to do if something appears to be going wrong. You should always tell the school if homework seems to be taking too long.

The school should also try to provide a quiet room where children who have no place to study at home can do their homework after school.

Choosing which subjects to study

In a big secondary school most pupils will study the same subjects for the first two or three years. As well as the 'core' subjects, they will be given the chance to sample a wide range of other activities. For example, many schools use the Rotational Craft Timetable (RCT) which involves all pupils, boys and girls, in the first two years taking short craft courses. These 'rotate' from needlework to home economics to metalwork, woodwork, technical drawing, etc. By the third year pupils begin to be offered some choice, taking a second language for instance.

Choice at 14+

It is when pupils are 14, at the end of the third year in most secondary schools, that important choices which can have a decisive effect on their careers are made. Schools must tell parents how this is done, 'including the arrangements for the making by parents and pupils of such choices'. This shows that schools are expected to consult and involve parents. Many schools do this meticulously. They produce very informative option booklets, they take trouble to explain all the implications of choices, and do their best to see that pupils choose a broadly based group of subjects that will 'keep their options open' for the future. One very common system is to make Maths and English Language compulsory, while other subjects are offered in groups, or blocks, from which only one can be chosen.

If your child already has an eye on a particular career or college course, it is essential to make sure that the right subjects to gain entry are chosen. Though it may be possible to make up a missing qualification later on this is not to be recommended.

Schools have a particular responsibility at this stage to promote equal opportunities, not just by seeing that all subjects are equally available to boys and girls, but also by making it easy for them to take 'non-traditional' courses.

Working out options is complicated and often frustrating for schools, parents and pupils, and they may all three disagree. Parents want their children to get good qualifications and may be suspicious of 'fringe' subjects. Schools want their pupils to take courses which they can cope with, and may under-estimate their abilities. There are always timetabling problems, and schools vary in how far they are prepared to be flexible about making special arrangements. Pupils may be influenced by dislike of a particular teacher, or by wanting to be with friends.

Parents may be reassured by asking for information about the qualifications and careers unusual subjects can lead to, and they may be able to reassure teachers by their commitment and support for a child wanting to take a particular exam. It may be possible to take a subject at evening class, though you will need the school's permission. Parents and schools should try to persuade pupils to take a longer view, while remembering that in the end, people generally do better at courses they enjoy. An A in Photography is more use that an F in Biology, after all.

In the end, when all the consultation is over, the school has the final say about which options a pupil can take.

Choice at 16+

WHERE TO STUDY

Anyone who wants to continue their education after 16 has a choice of staying on at school, moving to a different school, going to further education (FE) college, or a sixth-form college or tertiary college if these are available, or to an independent college. In some LEAs schools work together to provide joint sixth-form courses, so that a wider choice of minority subjects can be offered in larger groups. (Small sixth-form teaching groups are very uneconomical, and often not very effective.) The right to choose the place you want still applies. Colleges maintained by the LEA are free to students under 18.

Schools can ask for a minimum number of O levels for pupils who want to take A level. If the school will not take someone into the sixth-form for this or any other reason, the LEA must provide a place elsewhere, though not necessarily to do A level.

WHAT TO STUDY

A large school or a college will offer one year or two year courses in a wide range of technical, business and vocational subjects besides GCE. Look carefully at these courses, which usually have a practical bias. Many have equivalent status to GCE as entry requirements, and may be more useful in getting a job.

It is important to choose courses that qualify for entry to any intended career or higher education. Check with the *Compendium of university entrance requirements* for university degrees, with the *Compendium of advanced courses in colleges of further and higher education* for courses at degree level outside the universities, with *British qualifications* for professional and technical qualifications.

It may not be possible to take a mixture of science and arts subjects because of timetabling difficulties. You cannot oblige a school to put on the course you want, even if it was mentioned in the published information about the school. With any luck you will be able to find it in another school or college. It may be easier to persuade an independent college to allow someone without good O level results to take A level.

Secondary school exams

GCE O LEVEL/CSE/GCSE

Although the General Certificate of Education (GCE) Ordinary Level was intended for the top 20% of the age group, and the Certificate of Secondary Education (CSE) for the next 40%, they have always overlapped. Indeed, nowadays only about 10% of school-leavers do not have at least one O level or CSE. The intention now is that GCE and CSE should be combined to form a common exam at 16+, called the General Certificate of Secondary Education (GCSE).

Pilot projects have been running for some time, and the merger is due to be complete in time for pupils taking the exam in 1988. The GCSE will have seven grades, Grade 1 being equivalent to an A at O level, and grade 7 to a Grade 5 CSE. The syllabuses and exams will have to comply with national criteria drawn up by the existing GCE and CSE Examining Boards, and approved by the Secretary of State.

The GCSE will be available in most of the subjects offered by the old exams. In order to cope with the spread of ability in candidates taking the exam, alternative papers will be set for some subjects. For instance, there could be three papers set in one subject, one taken by everyone, and a more difficult one and an easier one that candidates could choose between. Another subject might have the same exam paper for everyone with questions that get harder as they go on.

The new exam will not rely on written exams that test memory, but will also test creative skills and processes. There will be more assessment of course work, and practical tests. The basic requirement is that all candidates should have the opportunity to show what they know, understand and can do. If this intention is fulfilled, GCSE will be a much fairer and more useful test of achievement than many existing exams. Some exam boards are already offering common exams, the GCE and CSE will continue to be available until the new exam is brought in.

The DES has issued a leaflet *GCSE – the new exam at 16+* explaining the GCSE to parents and pupils, which is available free from DES Publications.

GCE A LEVEL

This is the recognised qualification for getting into university. It is on the whole a traditional academic course, though there are some more experimental syllabuses. Some universities have a preference for the traditional subjects and do not always accept new subjects and syllabuses as being of equal value when selecting their students. A free pamphlet published by the Committee of Vice Chancellors makes this very clear. 'Some subjects are universally acceptable, some enjoy only very limited recognition, and some are scarcely recognised at all.'

There have been complaints that the A level grading system is unfair, because very few marks may separate Grade B from Grade D. D would not normally be a good enough grade for a university place in a popular subject. A new fairer system has been proposed, which is expected to come into effect in 1987.

A/O levels are offered in some subjects. Their aim is to allow sixth-formers to continue to study a wider range of subjects without the burden of too many A levels. General Studies is a popular option at A/O level. They count the same as O level for entrance requirements.

A/S level is another attempt to broaden the sixth-form curriculum. The Advanced Supplementary exam is planned to start in 1989, and will be equivalent to half an A level, so that a pupil might take two A levels and two A/S levels instead of three A levels. A/S level should not be confused with the Special (S) Papers some A level students take as an extra test of ability.

CEE

The Certificate of Extended Education was designed as a one year alternative to A level for people who had taken CSE. It began life as an experiment, but has been very popular with some schools, and resisted all attempts to close it down. The latest idea is to merge it with the CPVE, (see below).

CPVE

The Certificate of Pre-Vocational Education is planned as a new vocational qualification, for pupils of 17+ who have taken a course based on practical activities rather than formal subject teaching.

BTEC

The Business and Technician Education Council offer business and technical qualifications at certificate and diploma level. The BTEC

National Diploma and Higher National Diploma are recognised as equivalent qualifications to GCE O and A level in many entrance requirements.

CITY AND GUILDS

The City and Guilds of London Institute is responsible for certificates in craft subjects related to most industries. Schools put pupils in for these as an alternative to CSE and A level. City and Guilds also offer Foundation Courses, which give a general introduction to careers in agriculture, community care, engineering, distribution, etc. They have devised a general vocational preparation programme to help bridge the gap between school and college and working life. This course (No 365) is suitable for pupils in their last two years at school.

ROYAL SOCIETY OF ARTS, PITMANS, AND LONDON CHAMBERS OF COMMERCE

These all offer a variety of certificates and qualifications in office and commercial skills.

Other methods of assessment

GRADED TESTS

Graded tests are designed to be carefully constructed tests of stages of learning and achievement. They are similar to the graded music exams, or tests of progress in sports like swimming and gymnastics. Now they are being used with a good deal of success in subjects like French and Maths. They seem to appeal to pupils and increase their motivation because they provide a target to work for that is within reach. Teachers claim that they are more flexible and can test the abilities of all pupils in a way that traditional exams do not. The danger is that they might come to dominate the curriculum, so that pupils were always doing tests.

PROFILES AND RECORDS OF ACHIEVEMENT

More and more schools are offering pupils the chance to build up their own personal records of achievement, to supplement and perhaps replace exam certificates as the only record of five years at secondary school. A personal profile includes samples of work, results of tests and exams, a record of how a pupil has worked and developed over the years, and information about their practical skills and personal qualities. Pupils and parents usually have the opportunity to contribute to the assessment. The difficulty is to give the records the same status as public exams like GCE. The DES is sponsoring a series of pilot projects and several LEAs and schools already have schemes in operation. A system that records what people can do, and what kind of people they are, must be more valuable than one that simply tests what they know.

Who decides about exam entries?

The school or college decides who should take a course and who should be allowed to enter the exam. So they can, for example, refuse to allow pupils to enter for O level, and put them in for CSE instead. Schools can avoid this particular problem to some extent by using the same syllabus for O level and CSE, and making the final decision about entries after the mock exams, usually held early in the Spring term.

Candidates have to be entered for an exam through a centre recognised by the examining board. This is normally the school or college. If the school refuses to enter a pupil as a candidate, it may be possible to enter privately through another centre, though some exam boards will not permit this. The deadline for private entries may be quite early in the Spring term. LEAs usually pay all the fees for pupils at maintained schools to enter public exams, but schools may sometimes be prepared to enter a 'doubtful' candidate if you offer to pay the entry fee.

Although in theory it is possible to study for an O level outside school, you would need the school's permission for someone under 16 to attend an evening class. Studying at home, perhaps with private tuition, and entering as a private candidate is an alternative, but if the exam board does not allow this you have to find an exam offered by a different board, which would be on a different syllabus, and a centre that would accept a private candidate. Details of syllabuses and regulations can be obtained from the examining boards, which are listed in *Education yearbook*. Some reference libraries keep the syllabuses and regulations for the main exams.

What can be done about disappointing exam results?

When the results come, and they are not good enough, it can be a devastating blow to children and parents. What can be done? The first step is to consult the school. There should be someone there to talk to and to ask for advice and help. If the problem is a missed university place, there are many sources of help, for example, *The Observer* newspaper's student service. Your school or the education office should be able to put you in touch with the DES Higher Education Information Service which has information about all the latest vacancies.

RE-MARKING

You can ask for papers to be checked, in case there is an error in the way marks have been calculated, or re-marked, which involves a full reassessment of the paper. The rules about re-marking vary according to the exam board, but it always has to be done through the school or college, who will be prepared to ask for a re-mark only if they think a serious mistake has been made. Individuals cannot request re-marking. A paper will not be marked down as a result of re-marking, but very few people who appeal are marked up. One exam board estimated that about 2% of candidates applied for re-marking, and about 6% of them ended up with higher grades.

A school can ask for the papers of a whole class to be reviewed if they have all done badly. This can show up weaknesses in the school's teaching or in the exam itself.

RE-TAKING

You can re-take most popular GCE subjects at Christmas, or wait until the following summer. Schools vary about the help they will give re-takers. If they are not helpful, it may be better to take a full year's course somewhere else.

Many people think that a 'crammer', or to give it the proper name an independent tutorial college, is the answer. Their advantages are that they may be more flexible than schools; they are geared to passing exams; they may be able to offer a concentrated short course for Christmas re-takes. Disadvantages are that there is no quality control – anyone may set up an independent college, nor do the staff have to be qualified; they may not provide the structure and support that schools offer and they can be very expensive.

The Conference for Independent Further Education (CIFE) is an association of independent colleges which insists on strict conditions for membership, including an independent inspection every three years. Otherwise, personal recommendation is probably the best way of finding a good local independent college.

ACCEPTANCE

The third option, perhaps the hardest, is to accept the result and make new plans. There are plenty of courses at all levels which can lead to a worthwhile career. You may be surprised at what your local FE college can offer.

Careers advice

The Employment and Training Act 1973 makes it compulsory for LEAs to provide careers advice to people attending educational institutions in their area, and to keep records of the advice given. LEAs must give a summary of this record to school leavers, unless they received written statements when the advice was given.

Most LEAs do this through their careers service, which all pupils can consult, and by providing careers education in schools. It is fairly standard for all young people to be offered a personal interview, to which their parents are invited, with a careers officer, during the fourth or fifth year at secondary school. Careers officers may give aptitude tests and a questionnaire before or during the interview, as an aid to finding out what career might be suitable. LEAs vary in the amount of resources they are prepared to spend on their careers service, but most have a heavy work load.

Careers education in school is patchy. A DES survey in 1973 said that schools should provide:

- a policy of careers education for all pupils;
- a curriculum that keeps doors open;
- a teacher in charge of co-ordinated careers work.
- an effective working relationship with the careers service and employers and higher education;
- adequate collection and storage of information about all pupils;
- consultation with pupils, parents and careers officers;
- adequate accommodation and resources.

Unfortunately, very few schools have the resources to achieve this. There are excellent publications and materials available, the two most important sources being the Careers and Occupational Information Centre, (COIC) and the Careers Research and Advisory Centre, (CRAC). Most public libraries have at least some careers material, and some have special careers libraries. There are computerised careers advice systems, some of which are carried on Prestel, which may be available in the school or public library.

There are a number of private vocational guidance agencies which give advice on choosing a career, based on tests, questionnaires and interviews. These are expensive, but they have the advantage of being able to devote a considerable amount of time to each client. It is advisable to make enquiries about the qualifications and experience of the staff before deciding to enrol with them.

The British Psychological Society does not vet independent agencies, but it publishes a list of its members, all professionally qualified, who provide guidance services. This is available free with a stamp-addressed envelope.

The Independent Schools Careers Organisation (ISCO) provides careers information and services through independent schools which are members of the organisation.

HIGHER EDUCATION

Several organisations provide a computerised service giving details of courses and the qualifications needed to enter them.

ECCTIS (Educational Counselling and Credit Transfer Information Service), can answer queries on courses provided at universities, polytechnics and colleges through the UK and on all other further education courses in the south west of England.

Higher Education Information Service based at Middlesex Poly, can give information about courses in polytechnics and colleges of higher education all over the country. Polyscan, at North Staffs Poly, can give basic information about all courses at polytechnics. All these services can be contacted by telephone or by post. They are either free or charge a nominal fee.

3 Partnership with teachers

In 1967, the *Plowden report* on primary education said that parent–teacher co-operation was essential to the progress of the individual child and the well-being of the school. In 1984, the *Hargreaves report* on secondary education said 'For very many years we have known, both from well-established research findings and from common sense, that parental commitment is a cornerstone of the school's success'.

What progress has there been in those seventeen years and what rights do parents have? The law has changed in just one respect – all schools now have to have elected parent governors – but practice has changed very much for the better. The parent–teacher partnership flourishes in many schools. However, it still depends on the goodwill of the head and the individual teacher.

Teachers who are in dispute with the LEA often refuse to carry out any duties or activities that take place outside normal teaching hours. This applies to joint events with parents and to report-writing and report meetings. Teachers consider that these activities are not part of their normal contract of employment, but depend entirely on voluntary participation.

Parents' associations

Parent–teacher associations (PTAs) are now often known as School Associations, so as to emphasise that they are open to everyone interested in a school – former parents and pupils, non-teaching staff, members of the local community as well as parents and teachers.

There are still schools which do not have a parents' association. Some heads claim that a formal PTA can come between parents and the school, and discourage some parents from helping the school. There are no rules obliging a school to have a parents' association, and no obligation on a head or any member of staff to take part if there is one. Governors and the LEA can put pressure on a head who refuses to have a PTA but they cannot insist that one is permitted.

It is possible for a group of parents to set up their own school association independently of the head. The LEA may allow them to use the school as a meeting place. However, staff may be reluctant to co-operate if the head disapproves, and it will be difficult to communicate with other parents if you cannot circulate letters and notices through the school.

The National Confederation of Parent Teacher Associations (NCPTA) can offer a model constitution that helps to allay the worries of heads who are reluctant to have a PTA. Once the group is established, and is seen to help and support the school, progress can be made. It helps if you can find an issue on which the school needs public support, or is hoping to influence the LEA to provide some extra resources.

When you have a parents' association it is important to draw in all the parents. It is a common criticism of PTAs that a small group of unrepresentative parents can easily take over and alienate or exclude others. You need to be able to show that the association has support all through the school.

Parents often seem to be more willing to join in a smaller group, based on a class or tutor group, which has some meetings and activities on its own. For example, a school can run a series of form parties. All the parents of children in a class are invited, with the teachers who teach that class, to the home of one of the parents. The parents get the chance to meet the parents of their children's friends, and are encouraged to take part in school activities. These small groups can choose one of their members to serve on the school association's main committee. In this way, the committee becomes more representative of the school as whole.

Fund-raising

Most school associations are in the business of fund-raising. But should parents help the school by raising money for it? Most people would say 'Yes'. Should parents raise money to pay for essential books and equipment? Most people would say 'No'. Where do you draw the line?

The law says that the education provided in schools must be free, and that LEAs must provide the resources to give every child a suitable education. So if the LEA does not provide enough resources to teach the subjects on the curriculum effectively, and expects parents to make up the difference, it is breaking the law.

It sounds simple enough, until you try to define what is essential. If children have to share expensive text books, better-off parents may buy their children the books, so that fewer people have to share. But when the school is in a disadvantaged area, no-one may have any spare cash for books. Schools in prosperous areas may be able to raise more money than those in deprived areas. So should the LEA give more resources to schools in deprived areas at the expense of those where the standard of living is generally higher? This is bound to be unfair to some children. It helps if parents' associations work together in an LEA. However, the fairest and most sensible system is for the money to provide a decent standard of education for all to be collected in the form of taxes levied from the community as a whole according to their ability to pay.

This is not to say that fund-raising should be abandoned altogether. It helps the school provide genuine extras, it can get parents and teachers working together, it provides sociable and friendly occasions which attract parents who might not come to other meetings. Most schools would not want to do without it.

A school association ought to have its own bank account and treasurer, (with co-signatory). This protects the funds, and means that the association must be consulted about how the money is spent. It is surprising how popular the hand that holds the purse-strings can become, with the result that the association acquires some status in the school.

Communications

Any partnership depends on how the partners communicate with one another, so it is a pity that communication between home and school often seems to break down. Many misunderstandings could be avoided, for example, if parents were encouraged to keep the school informed about personal, family or health problems that might affect the way a child behaves in school in and out of lessons.

How the school communicates with parents makes a great difference to the way parents feel about the school. Often, schools seem to find it difficult to communicate in ordinary language; they fall back on jargonese. Here is a typical sentence, in this case from an infant school head's leaflet for new parents: 'Up to now she has relied on her mother for guidance and direction in the pattern of day to day experiences.' That might just be acceptable in a manual of child development, but it does not do much to reassure an anxious parent on a child's first day at school. A parents' association may be able to help, by looking at standard forms and letters, and suggesting how to make them more welcoming to parents. Most LEAs encourage their schools to send letters home in other languages where necessary, and may provide a translation service. Parents (and children) may be able to help with uncommon languages.

Because of the expense of postage, most letters are sent home by child post, a very unreliable method. Parents need to learn to check daily with their children to make sure that they have received all the messages. Some schools ask for an acknowledgement of important communications.

The information regulations (see page 13) set a basic minimum for communicating with parents, but good schools will do far more than this. A school newsletter, whether this is produced by the parents or the staff or both, is a good method of keeping parents in touch with what is going on. It can also carry standard information about how to contact the school, the governors and the school association.

The information regulations do not mention it, but it is important for parents to know how and when to get in touch with the school, and when they can come and see the head and staff. Schools are often not very specific. For example, they make vague statements like ‘Parents can come in at any time’, which can be discouraging. Most parents know very well that a head or a teacher cannot be free to see them ‘at any time’, so often they are reluctant to come at all. A better method is for the head or other senior teacher to set aside a regular time each week to see parents, and to make sure that this is publicised.

It is best to telephone to make an appointment, though some school secretaries, like doctor’s receptionists, see it as their job to put visitors off. Do not be put off if you have a legitimate cause. If necessary, send a formal request in writing.

Most schools go to a good deal of trouble to produce helpful information about the organisation and curriculum and school activities for parents. It is then up to the parents to take notice and respond. When teachers have spent much time and effort preparing an exhibition, a demonstration, a discussion or a seminar, it is very disappointing to find that only a few parents bother to turn up.

Parent helpers

There are plenty of good examples of positive ways in which parents can help in schools. It may be easier in the primary school, when parents are more likely to be free to come in during the day time, to listen to children read, for example. But secondary schools can use parents too, in Child Development classes, in bookshops, libraries, careers work, escorting pupils to conferences, interviews and visits. The ACE Information sheet *Helping schools*, by Rick Rogers, is full of good advice about what parents can do to help a school.

If you want to help in the classroom, you should be prepared to make a regular commitment. Children need to get used to visitors, and teachers need to plan their lessons knowing what help they can expect.

Schools that do not want parent helpers will find all sorts of excuses for not having them – lack of insurance, (not correct), unreliability, (can be planned for and coped with), favouritism, (the teacher as a professional should be able to prevent this). These are just a few of the arguments. The head may be in favour of parent help, but the individual teachers can decide whether to have parents in their classroom, and how they should be used.

Parent helpers are not replacing, but assisting, the professional teacher. This needs to be clearly understood by all concerned, including the pupils.

School reports

It is nowhere laid down that parents must receive a regular, written report or be invited to school to discuss their child's progress. However, the information regulations certainly expect this to happen, because schools are required to let parents know how it will be done. A school that refused altogether to report back to parents would no doubt be acting unreasonably. How reports are made, and how parents are consulted is up to the school.

In primary schools, it is unusual to get a written report except when the child is about to transfer to another school. Parents could expect to be invited to a parents' evening, or report meeting, in school at least once a year to discuss their child with the teachers.

Most secondary schools send a written report home each year, which usually includes comments by all the teachers who teach the pupil. Some schools send two copies and ask parents to send one back with their own comments on what was written about their child. All parents are normally invited to a report meeting in school. They can discuss the report with the teachers concerned, and talk to the tutor and head of house or year.

Some schools distinguish between report meetings and open days. Report meetings are solely for parents to discuss their child's progress. Open days are events when the school is open to visitors, who can wander about, look at the children's work, see displays and watch performances. An open day may not be intended to provide opportunities for talking to teachers about individual children. If parents think they have come to school to discuss their child, and teachers are not prepared for this, much ill-will can be caused on both sides. So the school should make it clear what sort of occasion is being arranged.

Report meetings can be rather daunting occasions. You may have to stand in a long queue to see, say, the Maths teacher, and when it comes to your turn, you cannot think of anything to say and nor can they, unless something is going wrong. The *Hargreaves report* suggested that every parent ought to be offered a half-hour interview once a year with their child's tutor, who would get time off teaching for this duty. They could then discuss their child's progress more fully, without worrying that they have other teachers to see and are keeping other parents waiting, (and eavesdropping). Some schools already arrange this.

In schools that use records of achievement as part of their assessment system, the report will go into that record, and can be illustrated by samples of work and comments on these from teachers and pupils.

A report does not have to be a collection of clichés that say very little about the individual child. If your school's reports are not very informative, the parents' association might be prepared to take this up with the school.

Confidentiality

A school report is a communication between the school and the parents that should not be shown to outsiders without the parents' permission. Because it covers only a short period of the pupil's school career, it may not give a fair picture of what the child is like. It should not, therefore, be shown to social workers or others asking for information about the child, except as part of a fuller record. However, since it may be included in the pupil's school record, parents should always write in to object to any false or unfair statement, and ask for it to be corrected.

Teachers are covered by 'qualified privilege' when writing reports. This means that they cannot be sued for libel for writing something derogatory about the child, unless it can be proved that they acted maliciously, or did not believe what they wrote.

School records

Every school keeps some kind of record on its pupils, often in the form of a file of information and documents, which may even include all the notes parents write to explain why the child was away from school, or to ask for them to be excused PE. Parents have no right of access to these files, though the contents may be shown to other agencies such as social services or the police without the parent's knowledge or consent. There have been cases of mistaken information being included in a child's record, which only comes to light by accident. Parents and teachers have expressed concern that the records contain hearsay and subjective comments, or notes on private conversations with teachers that parents did not know would be reported.

The Secretary of State has the right to make regulations about how educational records should be kept, but has not so far chosen to do so. Apart, that is, from the requirement in the *Schools and further education regulations 1981* that governors must decide how records should be passed on when a child changes schools or leaves school.

A few LEAs allow parents to see their child's record and correct any inaccuracies. Opposition to such open records is based on the fear that teachers might not be frank if they knew that parents would see what had been written. It has also been suggested that sensitive information, for example, about suspected child abuse, would cause offence or even a libel action. But as long as records contain accurate, factual information, and reasonable comments based on objective evidence, teachers have little to fear. They should surely be prepared to justify what is recorded, especially as it may affect a child's subsequent career.

Another area of concern is that the information in records does not always get passed on to other schools or teachers when it might be most useful. Now that this responsibility is given to the governors, they should make sure that the school is receiving adequate information from other schools, and is passing it on correctly. They could take the opportunity to ask the school to explain its whole policy on record-keeping, and to discuss it with parents.

In 1974 the United States Congress passed the Buckley amendment to the Family Right and Educational Privacy Act. This gives parents 'the right to inspect and review any and all official records, files and data directly related to them, including all material that is incorporated into each student's cumulative folder and intended for school use or to be available to parties outside the school system'. The most recent attempt to have a similar right written into United Kingdom law failed in 1984.

Records of careers advice

The records of careers advice which schools are obliged to keep (see page 50) are available to parents and pupils. However, pupils and parents have no right to see references written by the school for employers or for entry into higher education such as the one on the UCCA (university entrance) form.

Parent governors

The Education Act 1980 included a provision for all maintained schools, county and voluntary, to have elected parent and teacher representatives on the governing body. Many schools already had elected parent and teacher governors, and in September 1985 it became compulsory for all schools.

The 1980 Act says that all county, voluntary controlled and special schools must have two elected parent governors, and all voluntary aided schools must have one elected parent governor and one foundation governor who is a parent. This is the minimum; a number of schools have more.

The 1984 Green paper, *Parental influence at school*, went much further than the 1980 Act. It suggested that parents should be in a majority on the governing body. This was opposed by almost every educational organisation in the country, including all the parents' organisations. The main grounds for opposing it were that the governing body ought to be a partnership of all those interested in the school, and should not be dominated by any one group. The 1985 White paper *Better schools* withdrew the proposal, and the 1986 Education Bill proposes that elected parents should make up about a third of the total number of governors in county, voluntary controlled and special schools. No change from the 1980 Act is proposed for voluntary aided and special agreement schools.

What can parent governors do?

The parent governors can be a direct line of communication between the school and parents, though schools very much prefer that any individual problems should be brought to the head and staff first.

Parent governors bring the views and experiences of parents to the governing body. They cannot claim to speak for all the parents, but they can contribute a parent's perspective to the governing body's discussions. Parents know the school far better than most other governors, and they also have a sense of urgency – they know that next year may be too late for a whole group of children. A year is a short time to an administrator; for school-children it could be a tenth of their whole school career.

Although parents should go to the school first if they have a problem, it is often easier to talk about their worries to another parent. It may be the parent governor's job to accompany anxious parents to the school, and to some extent act as a mediator in any difficult situation. They should also act as a channel of communication between the school, the parents and the community outside. They cannot do this properly unless they keep in touch with all the parents. This can be done by making sure that parent governors are present at all school occasions, and that parents know how to contact them.

People inside and outside the school are more likely to speak frankly to them, when they might be diffident about making criticisms to teachers. But what parent governors should never be tempted to do is to run the school down to outsiders. This does no good, and can do much harm by antagonising staff. The proper place to bring up any criticism is at the governors' meeting. (See page 167.)

Election of parent governors

The DES makes three stipulations about the way parent governors should be elected:

- That the voting must be by secret ballot;
- That the candidates must be parents of children registered at the school;
- That the voters must be parents of children at the school.

The LEA or the governors of an aided school decide everything else about the election – who should be eligible to stand and to vote; how and where the election should be conducted, and how parents should be informed. The biggest problem is to encourage parents to vote at the elections, especially if there has been no tradition of parent participation in the school. This is why once the principle of elected parent governors has been established, it is equally important to get the election procedure right. Members of the ILEA parents' consultative committees, (see below), have drawn up a model procedure covering the points they had found to be important in their experience as parent governors:

- All main election meetings for all schools should be held during the same week.
- County Hall should arrange local newspaper, television and radio briefings before the elections to encourage interest by parents.
- New, more attractive election publicity material should be produced by County Hall and be available in different languages.
- Notice of a school's election meeting should be sent to each parent. Each child should write and stuff their own envelope. The ILEA should pay postage. The notice should give the date and time for the election meeting, date by which voting papers have to be returned, from where these are obtainable and how to get nominated to stand as parent governor.
- Schools should be asked to be sensitive to the needs of the parents when fixing the day and time of the election meeting.
- Schools should be encouraged to pay for creche facilities for the election meeting.
- Divisional Office should arrange for a current or ex-parent governor (who is not standing for office) to open the election meeting.
- The current or ex-parent governor should explain procedures and rules governing the meeting, ask for nominations from the floor for parents to chair the meeting, and nominations for two parents to act as returning officers.
- Nominations for the posts of parent governors should be allowed only for those parents present at the meeting.
- Parents should be able to nominate candidates in writing even if they are unable to attend the meeting themselves.

- Candidates should have the opportunity to talk about themselves at the meeting and answer questions.
- It should be made clear at the opening of the meeting on what topics questions may not be asked.
- After the meeting candidates should write, or have written for them by a friend, a short piece on why they should be or want to be a parent governor.
- The election addresses should be typed and duplicated by the school and sent to the home of each parent via the child.

  Also enclosed should be a voting paper which parents will have been told to expect in the original letter. Parents should be responsible for returning the voting paper to the school.
- Voting must take place before the first autumn term governors' meeting. Clerks should be instructed not to make any autumn term governors' meetings before an agreed date.
- Account must be taken of the particular circumstances of special boarding schools. Election meetings for each school could be held at County Hall, followed by a postal ballot of all parents. Travel expenses for parents should be paid by the ILEA and a creche provided.

If the parent governor's child leaves the school, the parent is no longer eligible, and the normal procedure is for a new election to be held. The new governor will then serve out the remainder of the former parent's term of office. Otherwise, elected governors may not be removed from office unless they become bankrupt, or are sent to prison for a criminal offence, or they fail to attend any governors' meetings for twelve months. (*School governing bodies regulations 1981*)

Help for parent governors

Parent governors often feel at a disadvantage because they are given no training for their job, and lack the structure and support that is available to political governors from their parties, and to teacher governors from their unions. In Inner London, the parent governors are better off, because there are parent governor consultative committees in each of the ten divisions of the ILEA. These consist of all the parent governors of all the schools in that division.

They meet once a term, and can ask for information and advice on almost any educational topic. They can request officers of the LEA to report to them, and can make representations on subjects of concern. They elect their own chairs, who all meet regularly at a central parents' consultative which advises the ILEA about parents' views. This structure not only supports parent governors, it gives continuity to their work, and enables them to build up expertise.

Parent governors who take their role seriously, and are prepared to devote themselves to carrying it out conscientiously, can offer parents the chance to communicate with the school while minimising the risk of personal conflict. With self-confidence, knowledge and a genuine understanding of what the school is trying to achieve and what parents want, they can influence very significantly the way the school operates.

4

Help for children with special educational needs

The Education Act 1981 took into account the many advances in the education of handicapped children over the last fifteen years. It focusses on the needs of the individual child and how these can best be met. The Act was based on the report of the committee of enquiry into the education of handicapped children (the Warnock Report) though it did not follow all the report's recommendations.

When you consider that it was only in 1970 that an Act was passed giving all children, however severe their handicap, the right to an education, and that in Northern Ireland some children can still be considered 'ineducable', you can see just how much progress has been made. However, parents of children with disabilities and difficulties still have fewer rights than parents of 'ordinary' children. They are often at a disadvantage because so many different agencies provide services, and so many professionals can be involved in one case. This means that parents do not always get all the services to which they are entitled, and do not know how to thread their way through the bureaucratic maze. Moreover, in spite of the vast increase in facilities, these are still far from adequate and are not evenly distributed around the country.

Some of the best sources of help are the many voluntary societies, often founded by parents, who provide information, advice, support and specialist facilities. You can find out about these from the Voluntary Council for Handicapped Children. The 1981 Act directs LEAs to tell parents whose children are being assessed for special educational need how to contact any voluntary organisation that may be able to help them.

Assessment

Many parents find that having their children's disability properly assessed is their first major problem. The system has improved in some ways since it was standardised in the 1981 Act, but parents and schools frequently complain about the long delays in getting the procedures completed.

Special educational needs

One of the most important changes introduced in the Act was the replacement of fixed categories of handicap by the concept of special educational needs. This recognises the fact that handicap is not static, that children can have learning or other difficulties without having an easily identified handicap like blindness, and that many children need extra help during their school career.

The definition in the Act of special educational need is:

> having a significantly greater difficulty in learning than most of their contemporaries;

or

> having a disability that hampers them from participating in normal education;

or

> being under five but likely to fall into one of these two groups on reaching school age.

Warnock suggested that as many as one in six children (around fifteen percent) having special educational needs at some time. Not all these children will require long term help, and very few will end up in special schools, which cater for between two and three percent of the school population.

How children are assessed

Most children with special educational needs will be catered for in ordinary (mainstream) schools, without any formal assessment procedure. But when a school, a parent, a doctor or a health visitor suspects that a child may have a severe learning difficulty, they can ask the LEA to carry out a full assessment.

If a child is under two, an assessment can only be made with the parent's consent. If the child is over two, parents cannot refuse to allow their child to be assessed if the LEA thinks it is necessary.

The purpose of the assessment, according to the DES Circular *Assessments and statements of special educational need* (1/83), is to arrive at a 'better understanding of children's learning difficulties for the practical purpose of providing a guide to their education and a basis against which to monitor their progress'.

The formal procedure

Once it has been decided that a child should be assessed, the LEA must give the parents formal notice in writing, with details of the procedure, and a named officer to go to for more information. The parent has twenty-nine days to appeal against an assessment being made. If, after all, the LEA decides not to carry out the assessment, it must notify the parent.

The 1981 Act specified very carefully how a formal assessment should be made, and stresses that parents must be involved at all stages. Any parent embarking on this gruelling process will find the ACE *Special education handbook* an invaluable guide.

Assessments must include educational, medical and psychological advice. Parents must be given notice of any examinations of their child, and told of their right to be present. They can submit their own evidence and comments. If they fail to send their child to an examination without good reason, they can be fined.

Language difficulties

If a child has difficulties at school because the home language is not English, this is not a learning difficulty according to the Act. Circular 1/83 says 'in assessing the child's special educational needs it is important to take account of the possibility that cultural differences may mask the child's true learning potential'. The Circular recommends that LEAs should make every effort to see that someone familiar with the cultural background is involved in the assessment, and that notices to the parents are in a language they will be able to understand or have translated.

The statement

If as a result of the assessment, the LEA decides to make a 'statement' about the child's special educational needs, they must first submit a draft statement to the parent, who can comment on it. (In professional jargon, the process of making a statement is often called 'statementing' and a child with a statement is known as a 'statemented' child.) The statement has to include:

- details of what the LEA sees as the child's special educational needs;
- details of the special educational provision which the LEA thinks will meet those needs;
- the type of school needed, and if the LEA has a particular school in mind, its name;
- if education otherwise than at school is required, details of how it should be provided;
- details of any other services or support to be provided by the LEA or by the health authority or social services in order to help the child benefit from the education proposed;
- the evidence, advice and information provided by the professional workers assessing the child, and by the parents.

This last requirement is very important as it gives the parent a chance to know what is being said about their child. If parents are not happy with the draft statement, they can put forward objections to the LEA. The LEA then decides whether to change the draft, issue the statement as it stands, or not issue a statement at all. If a statement is issued, a copy must be sent to the parents, with details of the right to appeal and the name of someone to whom they can go for advice.

Appeals

You have a right of appeal to a local Appeals Committee, which is conducted under the same Code of Practice as for ordinary school choice appeals (see page 21). However, there is an important difference. The special education Appeals Committees can only confirm the LEA's decision, or ask them to reconsider it. They cannot uphold the parent's case against the LEA in the way that an ordinary school choice Appeals Committee can. If the Appeals Committee confirm the LEA's decision, or if they ask the LEA to reconsider and it refuses to change its mind, parents then have a special right of appeal to the Secretary of State under Section 8 of the 1981 Act. The Secretary of State may ask for the child to be re-examined, (in which case the parent has a right to be present but cannot refuse to allow the examination), and may then confirm the LEA's version of the statement, amend it, or direct the LEA to discontinue it. Not many parents are successful. If you believe that the appeal procedure was not properly carried out, you could consider appealing to the Ombudsman (see page 172) on the grounds of maladministration.

Keeping your child out of school

If the Secretary of State turns you down, you may decide to keep your child out of school. The LEA has powers to oblige you to send your child to school or make other suitable provision. These are slightly different for children with statements from those for other children.

The LEA will send you a notice informing you that they propose to issue a school attendance order (see page 102) for your child, and inviting you to say, within fifteen days, which school should be named in the order. If they do not think that the school you name is suitable, they can ask the Secretary of State to direct which school shall be named. When the Secretary of State names a school, that school must admit your child if it is a maintained school.

If you still refuse to send your child to the school, you can be taken to court and your child may be taken into care.

Once a school attendance order is in force, you cannot change schools or make other arrangements for your child's education without the LEA's agreement. You can apply to the Secretary of State if you think that the LEA is refusing this unreasonably.

Waiting for assessment

There may be long delays while a child is undergoing the assessment process, particularly if the parents and the Authority disagree. Normally children will remain at their old school while the assessment is carried out, but if they have been suspended from school they may not be receiving any education (see **Suspension**, page 108).

Though the LEA can enforce attendance at school on parents, parents do not have the same redress against LEAs if the child has to wait a long time for a place. In theory, Section 99 of the 1944 Act gives parents the right to complain to the Secretary of State on the grounds that the LEA is failing in its duty to provide suitable education. In practice, the defence that the LEA is doing its best to find a suitable place will probably be enough to prevent the Secretary of State from taking action.

Circular 1/83 suggests that a temporary placement should be found if the assessment is taking a long time. This should be for a stated period only, at the discretion of the LEA. Another alternative is home teaching (see page 78).

Reviewing statements

Statements should be reviewed every year, and Circular 1/83 says that this should be based on school reports, comments from other professionals, and the parents' views wherever possible. Parents have no specific right to see these reviews, but the Circular does say that parents should be regarded as partners in their child's assessment, and that there should be frankness and openness at all times.

Full re-assessments would normally take place only if there has been a major change in the child's development. Parents can request a re-assessment, or it may take place after an annual review. There is one compulsory re-assessment at about the age of fourteen, if a child has not been fully assessed the previous year. This is to help plan for the child's future after leaving school.

Moving to a new area

If you move to a new area, the new LEA has to decide whether your child needs special educational treatment. It should receive a copy of the old statement from your previous LEA. The new LEA can then carry out a new assessment, or, if you agree and the old assessment was done less than three years ago, can use that as a basis for deciding on your child's needs.

If the new LEA looks at the old statement and decides that your child does not need special educational treatment, and you disagree, you can request an assessment yourself.

Children under five

Circular 1/83 stresses the importance of early diagnosis. Health authorities are given a duty under the 1981 Act to inform the child's parents and the LEA if they think a child is likely to have special educational needs.

The procedures for assessing and statementing children under two are not laid down in the Act. The LEA can decide how to carry them out, and what form any special educational provision should take.

If children are between two and five the formal assessment and statementing procedures have to be carried out. The DES expresses the hope that LEAs will give priority to children with special educational needs for nursery school and nursery class places. The Circular also refers to the importance of liaison and co-operation between health and social services, the LEA and voluntary organisations. LEAs can provide home liaison teachers attached to special schools, they can help to support mother and toddler groups, and playgroups, and provide teachers in day nurseries.

Voluntary organisations may provide pre-school facilities for children with special needs. The Pre-School Playgroups Association has a Special Needs Advisor who can give help and advice to playgroups.

Choosing a special school

The rights of parents who want their child with special educational needs to be educated in an ordinary (mainstream) school are discussed in the section on **Integration** (see page 75).

The provisions about choice of school in the 1980 Act do not apply to special schools, or to parents of statemented children. But the fundamental principle set out in Section 76 of the 1944 Act, that as far as possible, children should be educated in accordance with the wishes of their parents does apply to them. Unfortunately, the excuses for not complying with parents' wishes – that it would be inefficient or uneconomic – seem to be used far more often in relation to children with special needs.

The formal process of statementing, with its emphasis on trying to find the best way of meeting the child's needs, often disguises the fact that parents may have very little real choice about how and where those needs should be met. Presumably, this is why parents of statemented children were not given the same rights of appeal as other parents (see page 71). It is intended that the process of discussion and consultation laid down in the assessment procedure will give parents every chance to express their preferences.

The choice is normally between a school maintained by the LEA, one maintained by another LEA, a non-maintained school, or an independent school. LEAs naturally prefer to place children in their own schools. Parents may believe that, for example, a non-maintained school run by a voluntary society will serve their child better. LEAs may not pay for a statemented child to attend an independent school unless it has been approved by the Secretary of State.

Other problems may arise with boarding. On the one hand, parents may not want their child to go away to school, while the LEA may consider that boarding is the only way to provide for the child's needs, or especially in the case of children with emotional or behavioural difficulties, that the child will do better away from home. On the other hand, parents want a boarding school, and the LEA may be reluctant to provide this because of the extra cost.

In all these cases, parents will need to produce evidence and if possible professional support for their views during the assessment process. A voluntary society may be able to give help and advice.

Parents of a child with special educational needs who is not statemented but who nevertheless want a place at a special school can rely on Section 76, but have no formal rights of appeal if they are turned down. They can appeal to the Secretary of State under Section 68 of the 1944 Act (see page 157) if they think that the LEA is acting unreasonably.

Integration

The 1981 Act recognised that many parents of children with special educational needs wanted their children to be educated in the mainstream of education. The Act says that LEAs must arrange for statemented children to be educated in ordinary schools, no matter how severe their difficulties, if:

- the parents' wishes have been taken into account;
- the special educational provision that meets the child's needs can be provided in the ordinary school;
- the education of the other children in the school will not be damaged;
- it is compatible with the efficient use of resources.

It also says that those responsible for the school must secure that as far as possible the child takes part in activities of the school together with children who do not have special educational needs.

The movement towards integration received an unprecedented endorsement when the Fish report *Education opportunities for all?* was published in 1985. This review of special educational provision in the ILEA, chaired by John Fish, an ex-HMI, came out strongly in favour of ending separate provision for children with special educational needs. The recommendation was all the more influential because the ILEA is the largest LEA in the country and has always prided itself on the quality and quantity of its special schools and other special education services.

The 1981 Act does not give parents an absolute right to have their statemented child educated in an ordinary school. In practice, many LEAs still take the view that educational provision to meet special needs cannot be provided in most ordinary schools, or that it would have an adverse effect on the education of other children in the school. If there are places in a suitable special school, and educating the child in an ordinary school will require extra resources in that school, it can be difficult for parents to get what they want.

The Centre for Studies of Integration in Education can help parents and schools who want integrated education. It can provide examples of successful integration of children with every kind of handicap in many different areas. Very often, the first steps towards a policy of integration begin when an individual parent manages to persuade a head to accept their child.

Not all parents want integration for their child, especially one making good progress in a special school. Opposition is often because the child has had bad experiences in an ordinary school, or because an ordinary school had in effect rejected the child by insisting on a transfer to a special school. If integration is to work, it must have the support of all parents, (both those with children with special needs and those with other children), and the staff of the school and the LEA.

How can parents of children with special educational needs appeal for a place in an ordinary school?

If the child is the subject of a statement, parents should ask for the school they want when the draft statement is made. If the LEA refuses, parents can appeal to a special Appeals Committee as described on page 71 and can if necessary take their appeal to the Secretary of State. It will help if they can produce supporting evidence from the school about their willingness to take the child, and how they will provide for the child's needs, also from the professionals involved.

You will have to be able to show that the child's needs can be met, that other children's education will not be affected and that it will not cost more.

If the child is not statemented, you have the same rights over choosing a school as any other parent, and can appeal to an Appeals Committee which can rule in your favour (see page 21). The fact that your child may have some special educational need does not affect these rights as long as no statement has been issued. What you may find is that the LEA may begin the formal assessment procedure in order to forestall your appeal.

Special units

There are two main kinds of special unit. Some cater for a limited range of special educational needs, for example, the many units for deaf and partially hearing children attached to ordinary schools. Children attending such units are usually allocated places as a result of assessment leading to a statement. These units, though technically part of the main school, may in practice have little contact with other pupils. Governors have a particular responsibility towards children with special educational needs in their school so parents can press them to investigate how the unit can be integrated into school life.

Other special units are less specific, they may be called nurture groups, disruptive units, withdrawal units or some similar name. They may be on the same site as the school, or in different premises. One unit may serve several schools. Some are run by voluntary organisations. They cater for children whose behaviour causes anxiety, but does not appear to be difficult enough to require a full assessment and statement. Parents have no formal right to a say in whether their child attends such a unit, which may have a more restricted curriculum than the main school. The Fish report found cause for concern about admissions to these units in the ILEA, and recommended that the criteria for sending pupils to them should be clearly spelt out and parents consulted.

Parents who are concerned about their child being placed in one of these units should ask the LEA for the reasons for this. If they are not satisfied, they could consider asking for a formal assessment. This would give them the right to some say in the education the child was receiving, but could have the disadvantages implied in being statemented.

Home teaching

The 1981 Act reinforces the powers LEAs already have to provide education otherwise than at school. If the LEA thinks it would be inappropriate for the child to go to school or to attend school full-time, it can arrange for teaching at home, or elsewhere, for example, in hospital. LEAs may also provide home teaching in community homes and assessment or child guidance centres. The child's parents must be consulted if teaching is to be provided in this way.

Once a service only for children who were too ill to go to school, home teaching is given much more often to children whose behaviour is unacceptable in school. The ILEA has nine criteria for providing home teaching:

- physical – the child is unfit for school for more than six weeks;
- schoolgirl pregnancy – until up to six weeks after the baby is born;
- psychiatric – where a psychiatrist recommends it;
- waiting for a place in a special school or being assessed;
- psychological – where an educational psychologist recommends it;
- expulsion when the child has more than three terms left at school, but only until other arrangements are made;
- expulsion during the last year at school – home tuition until school leaving age;
- expulsion from special school – while the case is under review;
- other circumstances authorised by the officer in charge of special education.

There are no DES regulations about what should be provided. Depending on whether they are also receiving some education at school, most LEAs provide up to ten hours a week, (the equivalent of five half-days).

Home teaching is better than nothing, and many teachers help their pupils achieve good results. But except for the most difficult cases it cannot be a satisfactory substitute for full-time education at school. If home teaching is provided for a child with a statement of special educational needs, the arrangements should be explained in detail in the statement. If parents are not satisfied, they should make representations to the LEA.

Hospital schools

Providing education for children in hospital is part of the LEA's general duty to provide suitable education for all the children in its area. The hospital is expected to co-operate by providing facilities, while the LEA provides teachers, books and equipment, and any purpose-built accommodation.

If there are likely to be more than twenty-five children in the hospital at any one time, the DES expect the LEA to set up a hospital school with its own head and its own governing body. Hospital schools have to follow the same regulations as other special schools, as far as practicable. In Circular 4/74 the DES recommends that hospital schooling should be as regular as possible, and that the idea of going 'out' to school should be preserved, even if it only means moving to another area in the ward.

Many children will be in hospital temporarily, but they should receive teaching even for short periods, and specialist teaching should be provided for pupils taking exams. Arrangements can be made for public exams to be taken in hospital.

Circular 4/74 stresses the importance of encouraging parents to play a part in their children's education in hospital. They should, as far as possible, have the same opportunities for this as parents of children in ordinary schools. If you are not satisfied with the education your child is receiving in hospital, you should take this up with the LEA, and the governors if there is a hospital school. The local Community Health Council, or branch of the National Association for the Welfare of Children in Hospital (NAWCH) may be able to help.

It is easy for a child at an ordinary school who has to spend a long time in hospital to lose touch with friends, and with the work the class is doing. Parents may need to take the initiative and contact the class teacher or tutor who can be very helpful in maintaining links with the school.

Health Service support

The most recent re-organisation of the Health Service gave the District Health Authorities the responsibility for school health services, under the District Medical Officer (see page 124). The District Health Authorities provide support services like speech therapy and physiotherapy to schools, and may also arrange for schools to have their own full or part-time nurse. There are seldom enough therapists to go round. Some District Health Authorities are better supplied than others, and some are more generous than others towards schools. So it is quite possible for some schools to be better off than others in the same LEA.

If you want to campaign for more speech and physiotherapy in your school, it is the District Health Authority and not the LEA who should be the target. You may be able to enlist the help of the local Community Health Council.

When a child is receiving therapy at school, it is very valuable for the parent to be involved, as they can then reinforce the therapy and check bad habits at home. If they are not already given an opportunity to meet the therapist, parents should ask the school how this can be arranged.

There can sometimes be a lack of co-ordination between health and education services. Schools and parents complain that important medical information, which has a bearing on the child's educational progress, is not passed on. The best way to tackle this is through a joint policy, decided by the LEA and the health authorities, which gives guidelines to all schools and practitioners on how information should be communicated and on the rules to ensure confidentiality.

Access to school buildings

The Chronically Sick and Disabled Persons Act 1970 made it obligatory for local authorities to see that any buildings open to the public were accessible to disabled people, as far as possible. This included schools. It was reinforced by provisions in the 1981 Disabled Persons Act (which have not yet been brought into operation). Although it is stressed in DES Circular 2/82 that educational buildings should follow the requirements of Design Note 18, *Access for the physically disabled to educational buildings*, schools can still be excused from complying with these provisions if it is not 'reasonable and practicable' to do so.

It is disappointing to find that new schools are still being built and old schools extended or remodelled without having to provide access for wheelchairs. Local associations for physically handicapped people may be willing to support campaigns designed to improve access to school buildings.

If it is too expensive to make all schools accessible, at least one school in each area could be designated an open access school, with all the necessary modifications.

A say in school staffing 5

The quality of the teachers determines the quality of the school. How, in fact, could it be otherwise? Parents who are encouraged to work with teachers are almost always full of admiration for their skills and dedication. 'I don't know how they do it' is a frequent comment.

It is a pity, therefore, that teachers are often so defensive about their work; most of them have nothing to fear from exposure. When teachers are in dispute, and refuse to do anything except teach timetabled lessons, parents and the public begin to realise just how many other professional duties they are expected to perform. The dispute means that all reports, parents' evenings, games, out-of-school clubs and societies, school plays, school visits and outings come to an end.

There is no need therefore for teachers to resent the increasing parental involvement, especially through the governors, in areas like the curriculum, the interviewing and selection of staff, their promotion and deployment, and even, dare it be said, assessment. Teachers are more likely to get a fair hearing from parents who know the school well, than from outsiders whose knowledge of the school can only be superficial.

How many teachers can a school have?

The DES does not make any rules about how many teachers a school should have in relation to its size, except in the case of nursery schools and classes, where the ratio of children to adults, (including assistants), must not be more than 13 to 1. *The Education (teachers) regulations 1982* say that at any maintained school, and special school there must be 'a staff of teachers suitable and sufficient in numbers for the purpose of securing the provision of education appropriate to the ages, abilities, aptitudes and needs of the pupils thereat'. The regulations also say that the staff must include a headteacher. They go to explain what 'suitable' means, but not what 'sufficient' means.

It is in fact the LEA which decides how many teachers should be employed at the maintained schools in its area. This applies to voluntary schools as well as to county schools because although the voluntary school governors are technically the employers, the LEA pays the teachers' salaries.

What normally happens is that the LEA decides on a staffing policy, which provides for an overall pupil–teacher ratio, or number of pupils per teacher, which is applied to each school. The ratio may vary according to the age of the pupils. So if the primary school pupil teacher ratio is 25:1, a school of a hundred and fifty will be allowed six teachers. There will be some discretion about allowing extra teachers if a school can put up a case for them. A school with a high proportion of children with English as a second language, for example, could claim that it needed an extra teacher for supporting teaching of English.

The LEA has to take account of the Burnham system when staffing its schools. The Burnham Committee not only decides how teachers are paid, it also determines how many senior teachers and teachers above the lowest salary scale a school can have. The Burnham system is highly complex. Anyone who wants to come to grips with it should obtain a copy of the Inner London Governors' Guideline *Burnham and all that* (obtainable free with a large stamped-addressed envelope from NAGM, 22 Croftdown Road, London NW5 1EH).

So if parents feel that there are not enough teachers in their school they have to persuade the LEA that they need more. Governors can put forward the case to the LEA for more teachers in their school. Parents can campaign locally for an improvement in the pupil–teacher ratio for the whole area.

What qualifications do teachers have?

The DES is responsible for the training and qualification of teachers. No-one can teach in a maintained school unless they have qualifications approved by the Secretary of State. The basic qualifications for new teachers are:

- Grade C O level or Grade 1 CSE in Maths and English Language;
- A BEd (Bachelor of Education) degree or a PGCE (Post Graduate Certificate of Education) or an equivalent approved qualification.

There are special rules for long-standing teachers who do not have the specified qualifications. Unqualified teachers may be employed in special circumstances approved by the Secretary of State. Instructors are allowed to teach subjects involving art or skill, especially those connected with vocational courses, if they have relevant qualifications and experience and no qualified teacher is available. The Secretary of State has in the past also allowed graduates in certain 'shortage' subjects, notably science and maths, to be exempted from undergoing a course of teacher training before being employed as a teacher. At the present time, this exemption applies only in individual cases put forward by LEAs and approved by the Secretary of State. *The Education (teachers) regulations 1982* set out the rules about the employment of teachers.

Probation

Teachers are on probation during their first year of teaching. The teachers' regulations say that in this first year 'the duties assigned to a probationary teacher, his supervision and the conditions under which he works shall be such as to facilitate a fair and effective assessment of his conduct and efficiency as a teacher'. At the end of the year, the employer can record that the teacher has successfully completed the probationary year. The names of people with 'qualified teacher status' are registered with the DES. The employer may suggest that a further period of probation is needed, in which case the teacher can make representations. The employers can report to the Secretary of State that in their opinion the probationer will never make a good teacher. The probationer can appeal to the Secretary of State, who decides whether or not the report should be accepted. If it is accepted, the teacher may not be employed in any school without the Secretary of State's consent.

The help that a probationary teacher receives from the school and the LEA can make a great difference to their development as a competent teacher, (and to the children in their care). The governors ought to keep an eye on what is being done for their school's probationers.

Health

Students have to undergo a medical examination before being accepted on a teacher training course, and the Secretary of State can bar those whose health and physical capacity are not considered adequate for teaching.

How are teachers trained?

The Secretary of State controls the amount of teacher training carried out in colleges, polytechnics and universities. The colleges design the content and structure of the various courses, though the Secretary of State can decide whether or not to approve them as leading to qualified teacher status. The Advisory Committee on the Supply and Education of Teachers (ACSET) advises the Secretary of State on how many teachers should be trained and how they should be trained. The committee's advice is not always accepted. For example, in 1985 they predicted a much greater need for primary school teachers ten years ahead than the DES were prepared to accept.

The quality of teacher training is often criticised, particularly as regards the amount of practical teaching experience given to student teachers. The government's 1983 White paper *Teaching quality* sets out their proposals for improving the quality of teacher training, which include a greater emphasis on practical work. As a result of the White paper, a Council for the Accreditation of Teacher Education (CATE) has been set up, and its first job is to review all existing teacher training courses. It is proposed that local committees should be established, representing schools, colleges, the LEA and, significantly, 'individuals from outside the education service'. The committees will discuss local teacher training and will be expected to promote links between the schools, the colleges and the local community. Parents and governors could ask for representation on these committees.

In-service training

ACSET also gives advice about in-service training (INSET) for qualified teachers. It ought to be every teacher's right and duty to maintain and refresh their professional teaching skills, especially when so many new skills and new kinds of expertise are being expected of teachers. In the ACSET report on *The in-service education, training and professional development of school teachers* (August 1984), the committee set out recommendations on in-service training, including the comment 'we regard it as unsatisfactory that geographical location and ability to pay should be factors in determining whether or not teachers have access to INSET'.

The governing body ought to be aware of the in-service training facilities provided in their LEA, and what use the teachers in their school have been able to make of them.

How are teachers appointed to their jobs?

In voluntary aided schools, the governors are the employers and have the power to interview and select the school staff. In practice, this is often delegated to the head, or to a panel of governors. In county and voluntary controlled schools, the LEA is the employer and makes all appointments, but the right to interview and select a candidate to be recommended for appointment is often given to the governing body. The LEA can refuse to accept the governors' recommendation, or can refuse to approve a candidate chosen by a voluntary school governing body, if it thinks the candidate is unsuitable. This does not apply to some teachers of religious instruction (see page 37). The school's Articles of Government (see page 165) will explain what powers the governors have over appointments.

The LEA very seldom refuses to approve a teacher, as unsuitable candidates will normally have been weeded out at the shortlisting stage. When a vacancy occurs, the LEA decides whether it should be filled. If so, the post will be advertised. The LEA may have a policy of ring-fencing, restricting most jobs to teachers working in its area, because of falling rolls and the need to find jobs for teachers already employed. In that case, the post will be advertised internally through the LEA's own channels. Otherwise, most job advertisements for teachers go into the *Times Educational Supplement*.

Governors may be involved in drawing up the advertisement, and the job description, and in the shortlisting. Shortlisted candidates should be invited to visit the school before the interview. Heads will almost always take a leading part in selection and interviewing, and deputy heads or heads of department may be invited to attend the interview. The governors would then interview the shortlisted candidates and make their choice, usually aided by an LEA inspector.

Where the governors are not involved, selection may be done by the head, or centrally at the Education Offices.

Choosing a new head

The choice of a new head is normally made by a joint panel of governors and LEA representatives, though in some areas the governors are not allowed to play any part. The White paper *Better schools* proposes that all governing bodies should have the right to be involved in selecting heads and other teachers.

Redeployment

At a time when pupil numbers are falling, schools may be closed or the number of teachers in a school reduced. Surplus teachers will have to be found other jobs or made redundant. LEAs normally reach agreement with local teachers' unions about how this should be done. If redeployed teachers are given a post at another school this may conflict with the rights of governors to select their school's teachers which is enshrined in the the school's Articles of Government.

Normally, the agreement with the unions takes precedence, though governors may have to be consulted.

Appointment of teachers from ethnic minorities

Even in areas where there is a high proportion of people from ethnic minorities, they are under-represented on the teaching staffs of schools. This is bad for race relations, because it is evidence of discrimination, and because ethnic minority teachers can contribute to multi-cultural education and provide models for young members of their communities to identify with.

It is illegal to treat anyone applying for a job less favourably than other candidates on grounds of race, and governors ought also to be aware of the need to appoint more black teachers.

The Swann report recommended that grants should be available for students who might not have the appropriate qualifications or might not have a sufficient command of English, so that they could attend 'access' courses to prepare them for teacher training courses. Swann also thought that more should be done by schools to encourage children from ethnic minorities to take up teaching.

Equal opportunities

When there are not many women in positions of authority in a school, it gives girls a poor impression of their own prospects for careers and good jobs, and gives an equally bad example to boys.

It is illegal to discriminate against candidates on grounds of sex, but the fact that women are under-represented in senior teaching posts demonstrates that discrimination does take place. It is against the law to ask questions at an interview that may have a sexist bias. A woman teacher took the Wirral LEA to an Industrial Tribunal because at an interview she was asked about her relationship with her husband, and whether she expected to have children. Men at the interview were not asked similar questions. It was ruled that the questions were discriminatory.

Parents need to support the school in its equal opportunities policies, and governors have a legal responsibility to see that these are carried out in interviewing and selection.

How are teachers promoted and assessed?

The Burnham Committee has an important influence on promotion for teachers. All teachers start on Scale 1 after their probationary year. Each year's service entitles them to an increase in salary, an increment. Once they reach the top of the scale, they cannot improve their salary except by moving up a scale.

The number of scale posts, posts above Scale 1, in a school is decided according to Burnham rules. Each school, depending on its size, has an allowance of points and each scale post costs points. So if a school wants to give a Scale 1 teacher more responsibility, and promote them to Scale 2, that uses up one point. A small school will not have many points to play with, perhaps three or four. Because of the decline in the birthrate, schools are getting smaller, and so, following Burnham rules, there are fewer scale posts. Teachers' prospects of promotion and higher salaries are becoming more and more limited.

The individual school decides how to allocate its points. This is usually done by the head. It has an important effect on the curriculum, because if a school wants to encourage good teachers, or to attract good new staff to a particular subject, the best way to do this is by offering a good scale post. The distribution of points needs to be carefully planned. This is all the more difficult because the existing arrangements can only be changed when a teacher with a scale post leaves, or the school can persuade the LEA to squeeze out an extra point or two for them.

Although the head has control over the distribution of staff as part of the internal management of the school, the governing body have a right to comment on staffing policy because it affects the curriculum which they oversee. Many schools now have a shadow staffing structure, that sets out their ideal arrangement of posts. This has been drawn up in consultation with the governors, and is used as a guide when appointments and promotions are being made.

Teacher appraisal

Teachers have resisted external assessment of their work since the abolition of payment by results almost a hundred years ago. By threatening to link assessment to pay, Sir Keith Joseph is raising the ghost of that scheme, in which every child who managed to pass the standard tests (usually by learning the answers by heart) brought in extra cash for the school. Most people concerned with education are prepared to accept that a proper system of appraisal for teachers could be beneficial, as it has been shown to be in the Civil Service, the armed forces and much of industry. The arguments begin when awkward questions are raised about who should do the appraising and how. The teaching unions would prefer no outsiders to be involved. Others might feel that a system that was carried out solely by the teachers themselves might not be altogether free from partiality.

A system based on national guidelines and standards sounds attractive, but it would be very difficult to draw up and agree the criteria. It would be all too easy for such a scheme to become a mechanical exercise or a bureaucratic nightmare, or both. However, it is possible to devise schemes which depend on locally defined aims, and which are set in a framework of support and encouragement rather than destructive criticism. They contain a large element of self-appraisal, together with help in identifying and building on strengths, as well as correcting weaknesses. The best schemes rely on practical classroom observation, not on second-hand evidence. Above all the people doing the assessing must have credibility with the assessed. You might then find, as the Suffolk Education Officer reported, (*Education* 3.5.85), that one of the best features of their pilot assessment scheme was the constructive dialogue that begins to take place, changing not just the person being assessed but the whole management system they have to work in.

It is always much easier to test what people know rather than what they can do. It is in every parent's interest that a reasonably fair and accurate system is developed for testing how well teachers can teach.

How teachers can lose their jobs

Teachers in county schools can be dismissed by their employer, the LEA. The school governors can recommend dismissal, but the LEA takes the decision. Voluntary school governors can dismiss teachers, but not without the LEA's agreement. (This does not apply to some teachers of religious education, see page 37.) The Secretary of State can direct LEAs not to employ a teacher. Teachers can be made redundant, in which case the unions have something to say about it. They can be dismissed for health reasons. If the LEA or the Secretary of State has reason to think that a teacher's health has deteriorated, they can ask for a medical examination. If this produces conclusive evidence of poor health, the teacher can be dismissed.

Misconduct is also a reason for dismissal. DES memorandum 3/82, *Misconduct of teachers*, sets out five kinds of misconduct which could lead to dismissal. These are:

- sexual offences and violence involving children or young people;
- other serious kinds of violence;
- misappropriation of school funds;
- serious deception about qualifications;

- repeated misconduct or multiple convictions unless of a minor kind.

Teachers can appeal against dismissal on grounds of misconduct, but if their appeal is turned down, their name is placed on List 99 so that other LEAs will know that they have been disqualified from teaching.

The memorandum does not cover incompetence or inefficiency, but teachers can be dismissed like any other employee for failing to perform their duties satisfactorily. It is a long and trying process for all concerned, as it is very difficult to prove that a teacher is incompetent, especially when they have been employed for some time. The procedure itself is fairly straightforward, but it must be carried out systematically and recorded carefully. Heads and other senior teachers, and possibly inspectors, have to be prepared to give evidence against a colleague.

The LEA will be anxious to avoid being taken to an industrial tribunal, when the dismissed teacher will be able to call on the teaching unions. The disciplinary procedures set out in the LEA's staff code and governing body's Articles of Government have to be strictly followed. The normal course of events is to begin with a reprimand, giving the reasons for this, and putting it on record. If there is no improvement, the next stage is an oral warning, explaining fully what is unsatisfactory and offering help to overcome any weakness in performance. This help must be provided. If no progress is made within a reasonable time, the next and most crucial stage is a written warning, which may have to be approved by the inspector or Education Officer. This sets out the causes for complaint, the planned support and training to be provided, and the stated time within which the teacher must demonstrate an improvement. All these stages, including all the help given, must be recorded, so that the record can be produced later as evidence if necessary.

Teachers who are still unsatisfactory at the end of the stated period can reasonably and fairly be dismissed, if all the procedures have been followed correctly and without prejudice. The professionals involved usually dislike all this very much, and put it off if they possibly can. Parents may feel that their squeamishness is less than fair to the children in the school.

Class size

The size of classes in a school depends on three main factors: the pupil–teacher ratio, the amount of teaching time each teacher has and the way heads decide to use the teachers in their school.

When deciding how to use their staff, heads have to take into account the advice given by inspectors, the views of the staff themselves, and the influence of the governors. The layout of the school buildings also affects the decisions; it is difficult, for example, to have team-teaching without some large classrooms, or to have five classes in a junior school that has only four rooms.

An LEA may claim that its pupil–teacher ratio is 22:1. Parents are then surprised to discover that their child is in a class of thirty. But every teacher is counted in the ratio, including the head who does very little teaching. Senior teachers will have time off for administration, co-ordination, and pastoral work. It is not difficult in a large school for a disproportionate amount of teacher time to be taken up with co-ordinating activities and discussions. All teachers have an allowance of free periods, and time has to be found for in-service training, and visits.

In a secondary school, the head may decide to offer a wide choice of subjects in the sixth form, which may mean that the A level teaching groups are fairly small, and results in larger classes at the lower end of the school. Where equipment is being used, the groups may have to be limited in size because of problems of space and safety supervision. Popular schools may have larger classes than less popular ones, because every place will be taken up.

So if you are unhappy about the size of your child's class, the first step is to find out the reason. You may need to campaign for more teachers. Here the teachers' unions may support you. Several now have a policy of refusing to teach classes over a certain size.

You can find out how your LEA's pupil–teacher ratio compares with others by looking at the statistics. CIPFA, the Chartered Institute of Public Finance and Accountancy, produce statistics on every aspect of education spending, including teachers. These would be in a good reference library. You may find that the governors, and perhaps the inspectors, should be asking questions about how the existing teachers are being used.

Independent school teachers

The regulations about qualified teachers in the *Education (teachers) regulations 1982* do not apply to independent schools. However, independent schools have the same obligation as any other school to provide education suitable to the ages, abilities and aptitudes of its pupils, and must provide the resources and employ adequate staff to do so. Also, under Section 71 of the 1944 Act, the Secretary of State can serve a notice of complaint on an independent school if it is employing someone considered to be not a proper person to be a teacher in any school.

A school can ask for any complaint from the Secretary of State to be adjudicated by an independent schools tribunal. If the complaint is upheld the Secretary of State can withdraw registration from the school. It would then have to close.

Special schools

Non-maintained special schools have to follow the same regulations as maintained schools about the qualifications of teachers.

Independent schools approved by the Secretary of State as suitable for children with statements of special educational need have to conform to the same standards.

Teachers of blind and of deaf children must have specialist qualifications. Otherwise no special qualifications are required for teaching children with special educational needs, though many teachers have taken specialist courses and acquired additional qualifications.

Most special schools have more generous staffing than other schools, but there are no regulations about this.

Non-teaching staff

The non-teaching staff of a school, who may also be known as support staff or ancillary staff, include the dinner ladies, the school office staff, the laboratory technicians, the librarian, the caretaker and the cleaners, and the media resources officer (MRO) who looks after the video and other equipment. Together or separately they can have a very significant effect on the school's quality of life. Yet the DES is silent as to regulations about who and how many should be employed. No minimum standards are laid down, and the only reference in *Better schools* is a suggestion that governors should be consulted about their appointment.

The LEA decides how many non-teaching staff each school should have. Interviewing and selection may be done centrally, more often by the head. Governors may play a part in the selection of the school caretaker and some other staff.

It is not always clear to whom non-teaching staff are responsible. School meals staff report to the LEA School Meals Organiser, caretakers may report to the LEA caretakers' section, as well as to the head. The hours of work and conditions of employment may be decided by national union agreements.

Some LEAs arrange training for their unskilled non-teaching staff. This is valuable because it can not only improve their skills, but also help them to understand the school's methods and policies, and how to support them.

If you have any worries about any respect of the support your school receives from non-teaching staff, you should find out from the head who is responsible and ask the governors to take it up.

6

Law and order

In the past, when the legal system has impinged on education, parents have almost always had the worst of it. Education law as interpreted by the courts has sometimes seemed very remote from the real life of schools. There was, for example, the judge who in 1955 could see nothing wrong in leaving 48 eleven-year-old boys alone in a room where there was an unlocked cupboard containing four-inch scoring knives. Most parents might feel that the lack of supervision had something to do with the consequence that one boy lost an eye.

However, coinciding perhaps with greater emphasis on partnership between parents and schools, it does seem that the concept of what are reasonable precautions and reasonable conduct is developing in the parents' favour. This may be because schools more and more have to explain and justify their rules to governors and parents.

Attendance at school

The laws about attendance at school are intended to be a protection for children, to ensure that every child has the opportunity of being educated. The one duty parents are clearly given in the 1944 Act, (and for long before then), is to send their child to school or to provide a suitable alternative form of education. So during the years of compulsory school, 5–16, children must attend school regularly, or be educated otherwise (see page 7).

If the child is registered at a maintained school, and attends regularly, that is good enough, (no matter what the parents may think of the education being offered there). It may not be good enough for the child to attend an independent school if the LEA does not think that the school is providing efficient education suited to the child's age, ability and aptitude. It would be up to the parents and the school to prove that the education was suitable.

Registration

All schools, maintained, or independent, must keep registers of their pupils. They must have an admission register, that contains the names, ages and addresses of all the pupils in the school. They must also, except for independent boarding schools, keep an attendance register, which must be marked at the beginning of every morning and every afternoon session. If a child is repeatedly absent, or is away for more than two weeks without a medical certificate, this must be reported to the LEA. Pupils' names must not be removed from the register except under the circumstances specified in the *Pupils' registration regulations 1956*. These are straightforward. The most important is the regulation that a pupil's name cannot be removed because of expulsion unless this is on reasonable grounds.

Reasonable cause for absence

Section 39 of the 1944 Act sets out the acceptable reasons for not sending a child to school. These are:

ILLNESS

When a child is ill or has been exposed to an infectious disease (see page 128), medical certificates may be asked for but are not legally required for an absence of less than two weeks.

UNAVOIDABLE CAUSE

Apart from the very occasional emergency, the unavoidable cause must relate to the child, not the parent. This was determined in a case in 1949 (Jenkins v Howells) when a girl was staying away from school to look after the family while the mother was seriously ill. However sympathetic the court might feel to an individual case, the principle that all children have a right to be educated has to prevail.

RELIGIOUS OBSERVANCE

Children may stay away on days set apart by their parents' religion for religious ceremonies. In the case of Church of England pupils, the only relevant day is Ascension Day.

CLEANLINESS

Children who have headlice or other infestations may stay at home while waiting for treatment.

TRANSPORT

Under certain circumstances, the LEA must provide transport to school (see page 11). If the LEA fails to do this, the parent cannot be prosecuted because the child is not in school.

WORK EXPERIENCE

Older pupils may have time out of school for properly organised periods of work experience (Education (Work Experience) Act 1973) but not for any other employment except in the entertainment business.

ENTERTAINMENT LICENCES

Children who take part professionally in plays, films, etc, must have an entertainment licence from the LEA. This will specify the times they may miss school and the alternative arrangements for the child's education. A license will not be granted unless the LEA is satisfied about the child's welfare and education.

FAMILY HOLIDAY

Parents, or other people having charge of a child, can ask the school governors for leave of absence during term-time for an annual holiday. According to the DES it would be unreasonable not to grant this as long as it did not involve more than two weeks' absence during the whole school year.

What is full-time attendance?

It has been established in law that full-time attendance means being there when the register is called at the beginning of the session and staying all day. So a child who is persistently late and misses the register is not 'attending' within the meaning of the Act.

Once children are registered at a school, they must attend all the timetabled lessons. Parents cannot withdraw a child during the school day for private lessons somewhere else. The Chief Justice said, in 1929, 'It was never intended that a child attending the school might be withdrawn for this or that hour to attend the lesson thought by the parent to be more useful or possibly in the long run more remunerative. The timetable and discipline of the school could be reduced to chaos if that were permissible' (Osborne v Martin).

There are special rules about withdrawing from religious education (see page 35) and concessions may be allowed for some health education lessons (see page 40).

Parents have been successfully prosecuted for non-attendance when they have sent their child to school and the school has refused to admit them. If the parents refuse to comply with some condition the school has made, and know that the school will not admit the child unless it is complied with, then they are failing in their duty to send the child to school. This has been applied in the past to children whose parents would not allow them to be medically examined, to children who in the opinion of the school were dressed unsuitably, and to children whose parents refused to allow them to be caned as a punishment.

Prosecutions like this can only take place if the LEA is prepared to back the school up in its insistence on the rules, which must be capable of being considered reasonable (see page 104).

What is full-time education?

The Acts do not explain how full-time education is defined, but there are regulations about the length of the school day and school terms. The *Education (schools and further education) regulations 1981* say that the school day must be divided into two sessions, with a break in the middle of the day, unless there are exceptional circumstances. When a school is open six days a week, two of the days can be half days.

There must be four hundred sessions (the equivalent of two hundred full days) in each school year. A school may have ten occasional days' holiday during term-time out of this total. If for some good reason the school cannot meet for one of the sessions, and the time cannot practicably be made up, this session is not deducted from the total.

The school day must consist of at least three hours' 'secular instruction' for children under eight and at least four hours for children over that age. Secular instruction means all the lessons on the timetable, except special religious instruction. The time taken for calling the register is not included but any time taken up for medical or dental examinations, or short breaks for recreation at mid-morning, for instance, can be counted towards the total.

The timing of the school day must be shown on the timetable, as it has a bearing on the responsibility for safety of children in the school (see page 120).

The LEA may recommend standard hours for all its schools which may be longer than the specified minimum. It may be open to the governors to vary these according to local conditions. For example, if there are several large schools in the area, the times may be staggered so as to avoid congestion on local transport.

Parents ought to be consulted about any change of school hours, as it can affect their arrangements for meeting children, etc. They should make representations to the governors if they want to suggest changes or are not happy with any that are proposed.

What happens when a child is not receiving education at school or otherwise?

If an LEA believes that a child is not receiving a suitable education, it writes to the parents saying that unless they can show that the child is being educated, it will issue a school attendance order. Parents then have a fixed period of time, usually two weeks, to prove that they are providing suitable education. If they fail to reply, refuse to give information or fail to convince the LEA that the child is being educated properly the LEA serves a notice on them that it proposes to issue an attendance order, naming the school it proposes the child should attend. It may also suggest other possible schools. If these are voluntary aided or special agreement schools, the governors must consent to the school being named. Parents then have two weeks to reply. They can:

accept one of the named schools, or another school also acceptable to the LEA. That school will then be named in the order;

or

choose an independent school, and either persuade the LEA to pay, or pay the fees themselves. That independent school will then be named in the order;

or

name a different school which is not acceptable to the LEA. Parents can then appeal to an Appeals Committee as in other school choice cases.

The Appeals Committee can rule in their favour, in which case the school they chose is named in the order. It can rule against them, in which case the original school proposed by the LEA is named in the order.

If parents refuse to comply with the terms of the school attendance order they can be taken to court and, if found guilty, fined, or, in the case of repeated offences, imprisoned. The child may be taken into care. The courts have held that though the child may be well looked after, and not in any way beyond the control of the parents, the fact that they were not being educated was sufficient to prove that they were in need of 'care' (re DJMS 1977).

Once an attendance order has been made, it remains in force until the child reaches school-leaving age. Parents can apply to the LEA to have it removed or changed to a different school, and can appeal to the Secretary of State if they think that the LEA is refusing to do this unreasonably.

If a school attendance order is in force and later on the child again begins to miss school, the parent can be prosecuted immediately, without any preliminary procedures.

Parents who want to educate their child at home, and have failed to convince the LEA that the education they are providing is sufficient, have a second chance to do this when taken to court over failing to comply with a school attendance order. If they can convince the court that they are making satisfactory arrangements, the court may tell the LEA to revoke the order. The LEA can try again in due course if it still feels that the child is not being educated.

Truancy

In most cases where a child is not attending school, this is not because the parent wants a different kind of school or education. With or without the parents' knowledge, the child has decided not to go to school. If a child regularly fails to attend school without an acceptable excuse, the parents can be prosecuted and fined, and sent to prison for repeated offences. This applies even though they may have done all they could to see that the child attended school, or did not know about the absences. Instead of prosecuting the parents, the LEA may decide to bring care proceedings in the juvenile court. It will have to show that it has made prolonged attempts to get the child back into school but without success. LEAs often complain that even when persistent truants are in care, there is no guarantee that they will attend school regularly.

In *Fifteen thousand hours*, Michael Rutter and his colleagues showed that even allowing for difference in the pupils entering the school, some schools performed much better than others, on a whole range of measures, including truancy.

How a school responds to non-attendance is very important. Good schools keep careful records, follow up all cases of unexplained absence, (including those where the child registers and then slips out of school), and keep parents informed. In other words, they make life difficult for truants.

Before any legal intervention takes place, schools will be able to call on the education welfare service in most LEAs (see page 132). Their job is to find out why the child is absent, and if necessary provide help and support for the family, to encourage them to send the child to school.

High levels of non-attendance are a sign of something wrong, which governors and the school should be considering.

A few children suffer from school phobia, a fear of going to school which causes great distress to them and to their parents. It is important to get medical and psychological reports, and to explain what is wrong to the school. Otherwise, the school may take measures which make things worse.

POLICE AND TRUANCY

The police get involved in truancy because of its relationship with juvenile crime. But they have no right to detain children just because they are out of school in school hours. It is up to the parents, not the police, to see that children go to school. However, in some areas, police carry out truancy sweeps, rounding up all the truants and returning them to their schools, and most parents do not object to this, as long as it is done in a reasonable way.

School rules

Heads have control over the internal management and discipline of their school, and that includes the school rules. So if heads can show that a rule is reasonable and necessary for the maintenance of discipline, the governors, the LEA and the courts will almost always support them. In order to be considered reasonable, the rules do not have to be concerned simply with safety and order; as long as they are not so unreasonable or unusual that no other school would insist on them, they can be upheld.

The information regulations (see page 13) say that schools must publicise their arrangements for discipline, and how they bring 'school rules to the attention of pupils and parents'. This is significant because it gives strength to the view, often expressed by teachers, that if parents know what the rules are before they send their child to the school they cannot object to the way they are administered, in particular, the punishments used. To reinforce this, parents are sometimes asked to sign the rules when their child enters the school, but this signature cannot be taken to sanction unreasonable rules.

If you do have any objection to the rules or punishments, you should let the school know right at the beginning. It is unwise to wait until the issue comes up because of your child's behaviour.

The Taylor Committee report on school government, *A new partnership for our schools*, published in 1977, made the point that 'the best guarantee that high standards will be observed by the majority is a curriculum devised to give every child experience of success, and a structure of care which not only seeks to deal with any personal problems which jeopardise that success, but also makes them feel valued as an individual'. The report goes on to deplore the fact that 'discipline' is always taken to refer to indiscipline, instead of taking a more positive approach. They therefore suggested that the governors should formulate guidelines for the school 'which promote high standards of behaviour'.

This proposal was not taken up at the time, but the White paper *Better schools* proposes that the head should formulate the rules 'having regard to such principles and sanctions as the governing body may offer'. In the light of these recommendations, and as the governing body in any case have a duty to oversee the conduct of the school, it is in a strong position to make its views about the school rules known to the head.

Can the school impose its rules outside school hours?

It has been established since 1893 that 'the authority delegated to the schoolmaster is not limited to the four walls of the school'. (Cleary v Booth) This was a case where two boys were punished for assaulting another boy on the way to school. In a second case in 1929, a boy was punished for smoking in the street outside school hours. There was a school rule that forbade smoking in the school and in public. The court upheld the right of the school to impose reasonable rules ouside the school. This right is not unlimited, it has to be exercised reasonably, and any ruling on it would have to take into account all the circumstances. Schools could, for example, make it clear that taking part in racist attacks on the way to and from school would be punished by the school.

Schools would have a good case for making rules about what pupils can do outside school while wearing the school uniform. So it would be the pupil's right to join a demonstration outside school hours, but the school might prevent them from wearing school uniform at it, or indicating which school they came from.

Schools cannot legally insist on pupils taking part in games out of school hours, though they can, of course, make it very uncomfortable for those who refuse.

Forms of punishment

Any kind of punishment is an indication of failure, but schools have to have some sanctions against bad behaviour. The best schools manage with the fewest punishments.

DETENTION

Detention is the most common form of punishment in minor breaches of school rules. Keeping a child in after school could be construed as false imprisonment, but most parents will accept it as long as they have been notified in advance. However, if parents have not been informed, other considerations, including safety, are involved. As a result, the child may miss a bus, have to travel home alone for the first time, be prevented from attending a music lesson or other appointment, or be unable to meet a younger brother or sister as arranged. The school would be *ultra vires* in refusing to release the child to a parent who came to school and demanded their child.

To avoid all these complications, the school should comply fully with the information regulations, and tell parents what the rules about detention are. An acceptable code of practice would include the provision that parents would be given twenty-four hours notice, and could ask for another day to be substituted; that the child would be under adult supervision throughout the detention, and would be given a constructive piece of work to do, and that parents would be told at what time the child would be leaving the school.

CORPORAL PUNISHMENT

Corporal punishment causes more trouble than any other form of punishment. It has always been held to be the law that a teacher may inflict moderate and reasonable corporal punishment. (What is meant by moderate and reasonable is open to interpretation.) Because the teacher takes the parent's place (is '*in loco parentis*') while a child is at school, (see page 118), the teacher can inflict corporal punishment even when the real parent strongly disapproves. This is because corporal punishment is accepted by many people as being a reasonable way to punish children. A campaign has been waged for many years to ban corporal punishment in schools, or at least to allow parents to exempt their child. Some LEAs have banned corporal punishment, and not many schools still insist on it if a parent objects. However, the courts have consistently upheld the right of schools to punish children in this way, the most recent case being in 1985 when a mother was taken to court in the Mid-Glamorgan LEA for keeping her boys out of school because she refused to allow them to be caned.

This was in spite of the ruling in 1982 by the European Court of Human Justice that it was wrong to deprive children of education because of their parents' philosophical convictions about the use of corporal punishment. As a result of that case, abolitionists believed they had won the battle, but the Mid-Glamorgan case was won on the grounds that the philosophical conviction of the mother was not an 'unavoidable' cause as described in the law about attendance. It was also held that the judgement of the European Court was not binding on the magistrates.

In an attempt to resolve this confusion, Sir Keith Joseph presented a corporal punishment bill to the House of Commons. Parents were to be given the right to opt out of corporal punishment if it was used in a school. The House of Lords rejected the bill. The position about corporal punishment is still unclear. Most parents who are against it will be able to rely on the sanction of the European Court judgement, even in schools where corporal punishment is used.

In the meantime, the decision about whether or not a school should use corporal punishment rests with the governors, as part of their general direction of the conduct of the school.

Suspension

Suspension is widely regarded as another form of punishment. In spite of all the protestations that the power to suspend should be used sparingly, and that the intention of suspension is not to punish but to allow a cooling-off period while problems can be sorted out, there is no doubt that many children are spending long periods out of school because they have misbehaved in a way the school is unable to tolerate, though it may be sometimes quite a trivial matter.

All existing DES regulations say about suspension is that 'A child may not be excluded from school on other than reasonable grounds'. The Articles of Government of the school may not be much more help. They usually have a clause which says that the head can suspend a child immediately on any grounds believed adequate, but must report the suspension to the Chair of governors and to the Education Officer. In some cases, the head must consult the Education Officer first. Some LEAs have drawn up a careful procedure for dealing with suspensions which includes proper provision for children not in school, and a right of appeal to the governors. Others have made no special rules about what happens in suspension cases.

Even if no right of appeal to the governors is specified, parents can ask for the governors to consider their case on the grounds that the governing body has responsibility for the general direction of the school. Parents who want to appeal would normally be allowed to bring a friend with them to the hearing, which has to be conducted in accordance with the rules of natural justice, whether or not any special procedure was laid down. Teachers or governors who have been personally involved would not be allowed to take part, and the head ought not to act as both judge and witness. Even then, it has been questioned whether the governors, who have a commitment to the school, are the right people to hear appeals about suspensions. A fairer system might involve an independent appeal committee like the school choice committees. Schools may use suspension as a way of getting help in what they perceive to be an intolerable situation. They hope it will force the LEA to come up with a solution to the difficulties of a child who cannot cope with the normal school environment. It should always be a last resort, and should follow consultation with parents and other agencies.

Suggested code of practice on suspensions

There is at the moment no official code of practice on suspensions. However, the following points will give you some guidance.

- Heads should have the power to suspend immediately in cases where children are a danger to themselves or to others in the school.
- No child should be sent home before the school has checked that there is someone at home.
- In all cases other than where children are a danger to themselves or to others in the school suspension should only

be considered after attempts have been made to discuss the problem with the parents.

- If it is decided to suspend a child, parents should be given seven days' notice, and invited into school before that time is up to discuss what can be done to resolve the child's difficulties.
- The head must inform the Education Office immediately a suspension takes place, and must inform the Chair of governors as soon as possible.
- Parents should be informed of their right to appeal to an independent appeals tribunal.
- Pending an appeal or a transfer to another school, the child must be reinstated at the present school, or given a temporary placement at an assessment centre, some other special unit or another school. A child must not be at home without any educational support.
- Temporary placements must have a time limit, to be exceeded only with special permission from the Education Officer.
- If an appeals committee rules in the parents' favour, the decision is binding on the LEA and the school.
- In that case, the LEA and the school must draw up a plan, in consultation with the parents, for helping the child with any special needs.
- If the appeals committee rules against the parents, they must have a right to be consulted about any alternative arrangements made for the child, with a right of appeal against these if they are not satisfied.

Expulsion

Expulsion is not much used in maintained schools, because LEAs have to find another school place for any expelled pupil, so they discourage heads from resorting to it. Independent schools can expel pupils, but only on reasonable grounds. The case of Hutt v Haileybury College in 1888 established that a school was wrong to expel a boy on suspicion of stealing without any real proof. The court rules that to give schools absolute discretion about expulsion would be 'far too great and dangerous', having regard to the seriousness of the decision, and its effect on the pupil's future career.

As far as maintained schools are concerned, the pupils' registration regulations state that the LEA or the governors of a school can take a pupil's name off the register because of expulsion, but the parents have a right of appeal to the Secretary of State, who can reinstate the pupil if grounds for expulsion were not considered reasonable.

The decision to expel a child may rest with the governors, but they would normally have to consult the LEA.

School uniform

Heads can insist that their pupils wear school uniform by making it a matter of discipline, a school rule. The classic case is Speirs v Warrington in 1954, which established the principle a) that a head has the right to say that wearing or, in the actual case, not wearing trousers, was essential to maintain discipline, and b) that if the head as a consequence of this rule refused to admit a child, the parents were at fault and could be prosecuted for failing to send their child to school.

However, LEAs are more reluctant now to prosecute parents for not sending their children to school in uniform. Also rapidly changing fashions make rules about the length of hair, for instance, out of date before the governors have had a chance to agree them. Uniform must not be discriminatory as regards the customs of ethnic minorities.

Whether you believe that school uniform is an expression of the school identity, or an infringement of personal liberty, two things seem relatively uncontroversial. Firstly, no child should be made to feel inferior because of clothes, so clothing grants (see page 148) for poor families are a valuable resource for parents. Secondly, arguments about uniform ought not to be more important than the education the school is there to provide. It cannot be right for schools to refuse to allow pupils to sit an examination because they are not wearing the right clothes.

A good school will consult parents about school uniform, and will make it easy for pupils and parents to comply with compulsory uniform by choosing items that can be bought in any local chain store.

Confiscation

Teachers have a right to remove anything from children in school to which they object. Once the teacher has taken possession of the child's property, it must be kept safe, and not damaged or lost. If the teacher decides to keep an item for a while, to the end of the week or the end of term, it must be returned to the child in the same condition as when it was taken. (This would not apply to consumables such as sweets or chewing-gum!) Teachers who cannot produce an article when requested to do so, could be accused of stealing it.

A teacher who is reluctant to return a dangerous item to the child should make arrangements to return it to the parents. If parents ask for any confiscated item to be returned to them, the teacher has no legal right to refuse.

An increasing problem is that of drugs. If a teacher confiscates drugs from a pupil, these should either be destroyed immediately or handed over to the police. It would be advisable to consult the head at once, in view of the serious implications for the school and the child.

Lost property

The LEA and the school are not responsible for a child's possessions, even when they have been given to a teacher to look after, unless the teacher loses them through gross negligence or fraud, or fails to obey school rules about valuables. For example, if the rule was that all money and valuables should be taken to the office to be kept in the school safe, and the teacher had left an item in the classroom where it was stolen, the teacher would be liable.

A household insurance policy that includes a 'temporary removal' clause might cover expensive items of clothing like a new school coat, but you would probably have to show that no negligence was involved. You should make sure that musical instruments are covered by an 'all risks' policy if the child takes them to and from school.

An LEA might be prepared to make a good-will payment in cases of hardship, if a child had lost an expensive item of school clothing, or equipment used in school. The school or the education welfare service would be able to advise you about this.

More items end up in the school lost property box than are ever stolen or left on the bus. Children may be afraid to ask because they know they may get scolded by the teacher. It is always worthwhile asking if you can have a look for any lost items yourself. The safe rule is not to allow children to take valuable items to school, and to mark all clothes securely.

School property

If a child loses school property, you cannot legally be made to pay, though most parents would be prepared to contribute a reasonable amount if they can afford it. However, if the school lends your child a valuable musical instrument, check that the school insurance covers it, or insure it yourself with an 'all risks' policy.

Search

It has been claimed that it would be reasonable for a parent to search a child, then a teacher '*in loco parentis*' has the same right. But there is a considerable difference between parents searching a child in the privacy of their own home, and a teacher doing the same thing at school, possibly in front of a class.

Police who want to search a child are governed by the provisions of the Police and Criminal Evidence Act 1984, which came into force on 1st January 1986. They must have good reason for the search, and must not ask people to remove clothing (apart from a jacket, or overcoat, or gloves) in public. If they think a more thorough search is indicated it must be done in private. The Code of Practice accompanying the Act, which does not have the force of law, but is a discouragement to bad practice, says that searches may only be made by a police officer of the same sex as the person being searched, and must not be done in front of members of the opposite sex.

Rules about searches in school ought to be at least as stringent. A good school will not carry out searches for petty reasons, will not ask pupils to turn out their bags or pockets in public, will treat all pupils the same and will not single out anyone without hard evidence.

Teachers who do not follow these principles, and who search pupils in an arbitrary and unjust way could be liable to prosecution for assault.

Police in school

In many areas, police–school liaison schemes are in operation, where police officers come into school and give lessons about aspects of police work to the pupils. The aim is to build up good relations with children and young people in the hope of reducing crime. An HMI report, *Police liaison and the education system*, published in 1983, claimed that when these schemes were in action there was a significant drop in juvenile crime in the area. The report refers to the need for police liaison officers to be trained for the work, and suggests that teachers and youth workers should also receive training in co-operation with the police. Fears about police surveillance in schools may be allayed if parents, teachers and governors are consulted when a scheme is introduced.

The new Code of Practice associated with the Police and Criminal Evidence Act 1984, makes it clear that police should not come to a school to interview or arrest a pupil unless this is unavoidable. The head or a representative should always be present if this does take place. The Act says that the police should inform the parent or guardian of a young person who is being questioned or arrested as soon as possible, and this would apply equally to arrests and interviews in school.

Schools are under the same duty as anyone else to co-operate with the police and may not obstruct them in the course of their duty. The school should make sure that the Code of Practice is followed, and that parents are informed as soon as possible.

Police sometimes ask a school for information about a pupil. The Home Office has made it clear that school records, like social services files, are not open to police inspection under the terms of the Police Act 1984. Most LEAs instruct their heads to provide factual information from school records to police officers making an investigation. It is wrong for such information to include unverified or subjective comments from school records that parents may not have had the chance to see or correct.

Bullying

Bullying is a problem that can cause great distress to children and their parents, yet many schools tend not to take it seriously, on the basis that children have to learn to stand up for themselves.

However, teachers are legally responsible for the safety of children in their care (see page 118), which must include protection from physical, if not verbal, abuse from other children. The standard of supervision ought to be such that bullying in school is controllable. And if schools claim the right to enforce school rules out of school, this protection could be held to extend to journeys to and from school.

Perhaps the emphasis on finding out why a bully bullies has neglected the need to protect the victim. Helping children to come to terms with their own aggression, or lack of it, must be part of a school's responsibilities, along with the parents. The solution may be to involve all concerned, parents of both the bully and the bullied, and all the children in the class. Bringing the problem out into the open may make it less threatening and easier to control.

If bullying is widespread in a school and little is done to check it, the governing body's duty to oversee the conduct of the school gives them a responsibility to intervene and discuss with the school what can be done.

Disputes over custody

Parents who are in dispute over the custody of a child sometimes try to involve the school, perhaps by coming to school and demanding to take the child away. It is essential for the parent who has legal custody to let the school know about any dispute, so that the school is forewarned.

7

Health and safety at school

The Health and Safety Act 1974 requires schools, like other places of work, to have written statements of their safety policies, including the steps they take to protect pupils, who although not employees, are 'other persons likely to be affected'. The LEA as the employer, or the governing body of a voluntary school, is responsible for the safety of the buildings and equipment and the arrangements for using them. Schools must also conform to the requirements of the DES building regulations. The Act gives people in the school the right to damages if the employer is negligent, and the LEA (including members of the Education Committee responsible) can also be prosecuted for criminal negligence.

Generally, schools take their responsibilities very seriously, especially their fire precautions. Most schools have to have a fire drill at least once a term, which they must report to the governors. Though arson may be a hazard for schools out of school hours, there are hardly any recorded cases in recent years of school pupils being injured by fire.

Although schools are safer than most places of work, there are still buildings and workshops that do not come up to scratch. Anyone concerned about safety in any workplace can call in a Health and Safety Officer, so governors may be able to use the Health and Safety Act to put pressure on the LEA for improvements.

The teacher's duty of care

When a child goes to school, the teacher takes on the parent's responsibilities. This concept of '*in loco parentis*', in the parent's place, is crucial to much of the law about school safety and discipline. The principle was first stated in 1865, in the case of Fitzgerald v Northcote, when Chief Justice Cockburn stated that 'A parent, when he places his child with a school master, delegates to him all his own authority, so far as it is necessary for the welfare of the child'. It was defined more closely in Williams v Eady in 1893, when Mr Justice Cave said that the schoolmaster was bound to take such care of his boys as a careful father would take of his boys.

The case of Beaumont v Surrey County Council in 1967 extended the duty of care. The judge said that while it was reasonable to apply the standard of a prudent parent for individual instructions to individual children in school, this was an unrealistic guide for maintaining order and discipline in a school of nine hundred pupils. Mr Justice Lane considered that 'it is a headmaster's duty, bearing in mind the known propensities of boys, and indeed girls, between the ages of eleven and seventeen or eighteen, to take all reasonable and proper steps to prevent any of the pupils under his care from suffering injury from inanimate objects, from the actions of their fellow pupils, or from a combination of the two. This is a high standard.' This case is fairly recent in legal history, but cases since 1967 quoted in *The law of education* do seem to show that the courts are expecting higher standards of care from teachers.

The teacher's duty to supervise pupils

Beaumont v Surrey County Council also clarified what standard of supervision could be expected in a school. It should be good enough to stop a potentially dangerous game 'within two or three minutes of its inception'. The head is responsible for arranging adequate supervision in breaks and the lunch hour. This can be done by teachers, if they will agree, or by helpers who come in at lunch time. But whoever is on duty must patrol the area. It is not enough to be on call in the staff-room. Heads find it impossible to maintain safety standards when their staff are not willing to do dinner duty and the LEA will not pay for extra help. Then a head may decide that the only safe course of action is to close the school at lunch time, decanting the problem onto the street.

Even though a high standard is required, teachers are not expected to be able to prevent every accident. Other cases before 1967, where children had been injured in the playground in a way that might have been prevented if a teacher had been on the spot, were lost by the parents because the court found that the supervision had been reasonably careful.

Supervision on a school outings

Sometimes schools ask parents to sign a consent form before taking children on outings. This is a sensible precaution to ensure that parents know about the children being out of school and about any risks involved. If the school asks parents to sign an indemnity against any claim for an accident or loss during the outing, this has no legal force. Teachers taking children out cannot absolve themselves of the duy of care to the pupils in their charge, whatever the parent has signed. Under the Unfair Contracts Terms Act 1977, no agreement can be legally valid if it purports to take away the right to claim compensation for negligence leading to an injury.

LEAs usually make rules about the ratio of adults to children on outings, depending on the age of the children. The teacher in charge would be expected to bring primary school children back to school, not let them find their own way home. Older pupils might reasonably be permitted to do this, depending on their age and the distance from home.

Supervision of school journeys

When teachers take a school party on holiday or on an educational trip, they are '*in loco parentis*' twenty-four hours a day, and must take reasonable care of the children throughout the stay. In any kind of adventure holiday or camping trip, they must follow accepted safety standards, for example, those recommended in the DES leaflet *Safety in outdoor pursuits*. When a holiday activity involves danger, mountaineering for example, the teacher in charge should have the appropriate qualifications if they are to lead the party. The LEA will probably make regulations about the rules to be followed but, if not, parents should check that safety rules suggested by the sports organisations should be followed. The Central Council for Physical Recreation or the Sports Council will be able to give information.

School parties from the United Kingdom have a bad name in parts of Europe, especially in the day-trip towns like Calais and Boulogne, not because of lack of safety, but because lack of supervision allows bad behaviour, perhaps due to drink. The school may sometimes claim that these are voluntary activities put on on a voluntary basis by teachers in their free time, but it cannot disclaim responsibility. The governors should monitor the school journey arrangements and ask for reports on all journeys undertaken by pupils.

Accidents outside school hours

When does the school's responsibility for the children's safety begin and end? In one case, a teacher let a child out of school early, before the regular time for ending the school day, and the child was knocked down crossing the road, because the mother had not been there to meet here. It was ruled that the school had been negligent. If the mother had been late, she would have been negligent, but she was not. So schools have responsibility until the time set for the end of the school day.

There seems to be some doubt about the time at which the school has a duty to begin supervision. If children arrive at school very early, and are injured in the playground waiting for school to begin, the LEA is not usually responsible. The LEA or the school may make regulations about the time at which supervision is to start in the morning, and this would normally be ten minutes or so before the school starts. If children are delivered by school buses, it could be held that the school is responsible for them from the time they arrived.

Similarly, it was held that when a five year old child fell through a glass roof in the playground, a few minutes after the end of school, the school was not negligent in failing to provide supervision. If the children were waiting for a school bus, this might be different.

If the LEA provides transport, it has a duty to provide reasonable supervision during the journey to and from school.

In 1967 it was ruled that the LEA was not negligent when a boy's eye was injured by a pellet thrown by another pupil on the bus home. A prefect was supervising the boys, and it was stated that there was no 'unusual' larking about.

School crossings

The school and the LEA are not responsible for the safety of children crossing the road on the way to school. This is the responsibility of the local authority, or in London, the police. Motorists must comply with the signals of official crossing patrols, who should wear approved uniform and carry an approved sign. It is not always easy to recruit crossing patrols, and parents may be allowed to undertake the job. They must wear the correct uniform, and carry the standard sign. They must have the same training as other crossing patrols.

If parents think their school needs a crossing patrol, they have to convince the local authority or police. This may require a lengthy campaign, involving traffic surveys, lobbying local councillors, and getting signatures to petitions. Other possibilities are a traffic island, and traffic markings outside the school. When most parents bring their children to school by car there are always some careless parents who park on the yellow lines, block the view of children crossing and so on. One school had campaigned for years about this, and finally solved it by the simple expedient of getting police permission to put out no-parking cones during the morning and afternoon delivery and collection times. This succeeded when polite exhortation and angry recrimination had failed.

Negligence

It is not easy to prove that a teacher has been negligent and caused an accident. Teachers' unions are quick to defend their members against such a charge. The LEA, as the employer, or the governors of a voluntary school, are responsible for safety, so they can be sued for the negligent actions of their employees. To prove that negligence occurred, the parent must be able to show:

- that the child was in the school's care at the time. So the accident must have happened in normal school hours, or on an outing or school transport. This would include the dinner hour if the child was supposed to be in school;
- that the school had not provided reasonable supervision or that the school premises were unsafe;
- that the accident resulted from the school's failure and was not due to the extraordinary misbehaviour of the child.

If a child is seriously hurt in an accident in school, for which no-one is to blame, the child is not entitled to compensation. This risk can be covered by a personal accident insurance policy.

Coping with an accident

One of the requirements of the Health and Safety Act is that every work place should have at least one person qualified to administer first aid, and that the whereabouts of this person and first aid equipment should be clearly signposted.

If a child has to be taken to hospital, the parents should be informed as soon as possible. A responsible person should go with the child, and remain until the parent arrives or a doctor says the child can go home.

First aid for teeth

Many parents and teachers do not realise that a tooth which has been knocked out may be saved if it can be kept moist and warm (not hot) and the child got to the dentist within about half an hour. It is worth trying for a front tooth that is not a milk tooth.

Safety at playschemes and playcentres

Although holiday playschemes and after school playcentres may often be run at schools, and school staff may work in them, they are not the school's responsibility. They are usually run by the Youth Service which, though it may belong to the LEA, has an entirely separate administration in most LEAs. Voluntary organisations may provide playschemes with the help of LEA grants. The staff of a playscheme or playcentre have to provide the same standard of care as teachers.

If you have a worry about how these schemes operate, it can be quite difficult to track down who is responsible. The Area Youth Committee may in theory oversee those run by the Youth Service or those given LEA grants, but they are unlikely to have the time to investigate small individual schemes. They should however be prepared to take seriously any worries about safety.

Play Board is an organisation which co-ordinates the work of statutory and voluntary organisations working to provide play facilities for children. It collects and disseminates ideas and information, and can advise on all aspects of play and playschemes, especially safety. They have just set up a Safety Task Group.

The school health service

Old stagers say that the school health service has never been as good since it was taken away from the LEAs and given to the National Health Service. Since that happened in 1974, responsibility has passed from the Area Health Authorities, which were abolished in 1982, to the District Health Authorities, (DHAs). The District Medical Officer has overall responsibility for all child health services. Most DHAs cover only a part of an LEA area. The DHA are responsible for medical inspections in schools, and some services in clinics. They also provide eyesight and hearing tests, and dental services.

The future of the school health service is under discussion. Traditionally, child health services have been split three ways. Primary health care has been provided by GPs who do some preventive work but mainly carry out treatment of minor ailments, and by the health clinics and school health service who do some treatment and most of the preventive work. Secondary care of serious illness is provided by hospitals. The Court report recommended in 1976 that there should be an integrated service for primary care. GPs support this. The result might be that the GP would be the source for most of the preventive work now done in schools, as well as treatment.

At present, the LEA has a duty to encourage and assist pupils to take advantage of the provision of medical and dental inspection and treatment made by the DHA. If parents do not want to use the school health service, they are not obliged to do so.

Medical examinations

It is up to the DHA what services they decide to offer schools, but the DHSS recommends that all children should have a medical examination when they start school, and at appropriate intervals afterwards. The trend now is for children's health to be kept under review annually by the school nurse or doctor, and examinations to be made only of those children who give cause for concern. Parents should be notified when the examinations are to take place, and given the opportunity to attend. The DHA makes the arrangements, not the school, though it may be the school who notifies parents.

The DHSS also recommends that all children should have regular dental inspections.

If medical or dental treatment is needed, the DHA should offer school health facilities, though parents can make their own arrangements if they wish. Medical and dental records should be kept on all school children.

Parents should be able to ask for a school medical examination if they are worried about their child.

Eyesight tests

A basic eyesight test including a test for colour blindness is usually carried out when a child starts school. Children can then be referred to a specialist if there seems to be something wrong. It is a very simple test, so if parents are still concerned about their child's sight they should ask for a full examination through their GP. There is no charge for this, nor for spectacles for children under sixteen, or under nineteen if they are still in full-time education.

Hearing tests

Most children are given a hearing test on proper equipment during their early years at school. Do not wait for this if you think your child may have some hearing loss, as this can affect their educational progress very considerably.

Parents are not usually notified about routine sight and hearing tests, so let the school know in advance if you have a special reason for wanting to be present.

The school nurse will also carry out occasional inspections of hair, feet, etc. These may offend against the customs of some ethnic minority groups. Parents should tell the school if this is the case.

Schools should take steps to find out what is acceptable, and to make sure that all parents understand why the inspections need to be carried out.

School health service staff

As well as the therapists discussed in Chapter 4 on children with special needs, other staff employed by the District Health Authorities will be working full or part-time for the education service. In most areas, schools will have their own designated school doctor, who will carry out medical examinations, and can be called on for advice, especially for children with special educational needs. Depending on the size and type of the school, there may be a full-time or part-time school nurse, who will carry out minor medical procedures and inspections, and be available to give help and advice. The school doctor and the school nurse will be involved in the assessment of children with special needs.

Vaccinations

Most District Health Authorities offer a programme of vaccinations to school children. This is a convenient way of making sure that your child gets the recommended immunisations, but if you would prefer the family doctor to do these, or do not wish the child to be immunised, you should inform the school. They should let you know when the vaccinations are taking place. See table for the recommended schedule.

AGE	VACCINE	COMMENTS
5	Booster polio and double vaccine (diphtheria/ tetanus)	Should be done three years after earlier dose
11–13	BCG (TB)	For tuberculin negative children after BCG test

AGE	VACCINE	COMMENTS
11–13	Rubella (German Measles)	Girls only, at three weeks after BCG
On leaving school	Polio and Tetanus	

Although the health authorities can provide an immunisation service to independent schools this is not always done, so parents should make sure they do not miss the various recommended vaccinations.

Cleansing

LEAs have the power to insist on a medical examination if they suspect a child has some kind of infestation, like headlice, can arrange treatment, and can prohibit children from attending school until the treatment is carried out. Parents can make their own arrangements if they wish. If children are in a 'foul' condition, the LEA can insist on them and their clothing being cleaned, and must offer facilities for doing this. It is unfortunate that infestation and cleansing are always linked in the education acts, because the cleanest child in the school can easily pick up nits or worms from other children. You can buy a treatment from the local chemist, who will be quite used to supplying it. It is essential to treat everyone in the family and disinfect bedding, (duvets for example), or the child will quickly become reinfected.

The Health Education Council has a helpful pamphlet reassuring parents about infestation, and explaining what should be done.

If a child is dirty again, or is reinfected and has to stay away from school, and this can be proved to be the parent's fault, (not just due to reinfection in school), the parent can be prosecuted under the attendance regulations.

The days when a child could be prevented from going on a school journey because of verrucae are past, since modern methods of treatment make it much less necessary for children to be kept out of school. The 1977 DHSS/DES Memorandum *Control of communicable disease in schools*, intended for doctors, explains what the rules are.

Illness

How can a parent tell whether a child is well enough to go to school? Parents are all too familiar with the PE morning stomach-ache, or the haven't done homework temperature. The problem is how to distinguish between physical and psychosomatic illness, and what to do about it.

A child who suffers from persistent headaches or sickness ought to see the GP, but if nothing seems to be organically wrong, that does not mean the pain is not real. If the problem can be traced to school, the school may be able to help. Just talking about it may make the child feel better.

School phobia is more serious than a reluctance to go to school because you do not get on with the English teacher. A child who is genuinely terrified of going to school needs professional help. Some GPs are unsympathetic, in which case you should ask for referral to a consultant. If the child persistently and determinedly refuses to go to school you should ask for a medical certificate that will explain that the child is unfit for school. Most cases of school phobia, sympathetically handled, can be overcome. The LEA may be prepared to provide home teaching for a while (see page 78).

Infectious diseases

The DHSS recommends periods of exclusion from school for children who have had or have been exposed to infectious diseases, (*Control of communicable disease in schools*). The District Health Authority will decide what the local rules should be and has the right to exclude children, even if they appear to have recovered, for the stated period. For the common childhood ailments, children are not expected to stay at home if they have been in contact with the disease. German measles (rubella) is an exception, because it can be dangerous for pregnant women. The school should be informed about cases or contacts, and should warn parents if this disease is around.

Diarrhoea and food poisoning

The DHSS says that all illnesses that could possibly be attributed to school meals should be reported to the District Health Authority, even if they do not appear to be serious. So parents should let the school know about any stomach upsets.

Hygiene is an important factor in many stomach troubles, and children should be taught good personal hygiene, as the DHSS says 'through washing and drying of hands WITHOUT SHARING WATER OR TOWELS after visits to the toilet', (their capitals). LEAs should note the need for proper washing facilities in school cloakrooms.

School toilets are a constant source of worry to the staff, the governors, the parents, the pupils, the LEA and, above all, the cleaners. Inadequate, easily vandalised, often disgusting, they seem to pose an insoluble problem. Given that resources are limited, the first step towards tackling the problem is to make someone personally responsible. One anti-vandalism project involved pupils and cleaners working together in a concerted effort to keep the toilets clean after they had been redecorated and refitted. Because the pupils were involved, they exerted influence on their fellows to prevent damage, or to rectify it when it was done. The difficulty is to maintain interest in projects like this long enough to bring about a permanent change of attitude. And you have to start with facilities that are worth taking care of.

Asbestos

Asbestos was commonly used for insulating school buildings during the early '60s, before it was understood to be potentially dangerous. There are three kinds of asbestos: blue, brown and white. White is the most common. Blue asbestos is known to cause disease, but there is some doubt as to whether the others are also hazardous.

Under normal circumstances, asbestos is harmless, but when it is damaged, it may break down into very small fibres which can cause lung and other diseases. Now that the danger is known, blue asbestos is no longer used, and the use of the other kinds is restricted except where there is no practical substitute. The danger of damage can be reduced by sealing the asbestos material with special paint, or covering it with a suitable material.

Most LEAs have strict guidelines about safety precautions in the use of asbestos. These may be more stringent than those for industries where people are actually working with the mineral. The ILEA, for example, insists that 75% of air samples taken in a school must have less than 0.01 fibres per millilitre of air (about half an inch square) and no sample must contain more than 0.04 fibres.

If there is cause for concern, and sealing off the asbestos is not feasible, all the asbestos will have to be removed, and the air purified. Asbestos may have been used as lagging for pipes behind floors and walls and throughout the roof area, so it is easy to see how expensive the process of removal can be, and how long it is likely to take. If it is not possible to seal off parts of the school while work is going on, the whole school may have to close. The disruption caused may be out of all proportion to the actual health risk.

Sometimes the risk of disturbing asbestos in the hidden areas of the school building may prevent the LEA from investigating the possibility of improvements, for example to the heating system or the roof.

Until the medical and technical implications of using asbestos are fully understood, LEAs have difficult decisions to take. Removing all asbestos from every school could cost millions of pounds, for a risk that cannot be quantified. Pupils, parents and staff are understandably worried when asbestos fibres are found in their school. Rumours and exaggerations can cause great distress. So it is important that they should be kept fully informed and consulted from the start. Any temporary closure of a school causes disruption to school life. What to do depends on the options available, but experience does seem to show that it is better for morale to keep the school going on its own site, using Portacabins if necessary, rather than bus the pupils to other schools or makeshift accommodation elsewhere.

Schools' psychological service

All LEAs employ educational psychologists, who are qualified psychologists with a teaching qualification and some further special training. Some LEAs have a large and well-developed service, others may just employ the minimum of educational psychologists needed for assessing special needs and behaviour problems.

Even in the best LEAs, there is always a shortage of educational psychologists, but in a well-staffed service, staff members will provide advice and assistance to schools about child psychology and the nature of learning and behaviour difficulties, as well as being very much involved in the assessment of learning and behaviour difficulties, and in advising on how to treat them. They may also work in special units, child guidance centres and assessment centres, run either by the LEA or by health and social services and voluntary organisations.

The 1981 Act has had the effect of increasing their workload very considerably. They are involved in the assessment process, and are responsible for compiling the draft statement. Delays in obtaining the report of the educational psychologist are a frequent cause for complaint, not just for statements but for other children with less serious behavioural problems.

Child guidance clinics

Child guidance clinics may be run by the LEA or the local authority, or by the District Health Authority, in which case they may be attached to a hospital. They provide day treatment for children with psychiatric, emotional or behaviour problems, and are staffed by psychiatrists, educational psychologists, and social workers. Parents can ask for their child to be referred through the school, their GP, the Educational Welfare Service, or a hospital, or they may be able to ask for an appointment direct. Children cannot be treated at a child guidance centre without their parents' consent.

Children who go to a centre receive a full examination of their educational, emotional and psychological development. This assesses the personality and abilities of the child, and his or her relationships with others. Individual programmes of teaching and therapy are drawn up as a result of the assessment, usually in consultation with parents. Some clinics expect the family to attend the clinic and be fully involved with the treatment, others will expect to have the parents' support, but prefer to treat children on their own.

Child guidance clinics are unequally distributed around the country, and even in London, which is more generously provided than most areas, they are insufficient to meet the demand. There may be a long wait for an appointment.

Education welfare service

It is not compulsory for LEAs to have an education welfare service, but most of them do. The function of the education welfare officer (EWO) is to work with children and parents so that they can get the best out of the education system. Encouraging children to attend school regularly is only one part of this. Another important function is to build up good relations between the parents and the school, and to help parents obtain the educational services available to them. The EWO can explain how the system works and help parents apply for travel passes, free school meals, clothing and other grants. One description of reasons for calling on the Education Welfare Officer says: 'a marked deterioration in the standard of a pupil's work; a similar deterioration in behaviour; isolation in class; persistent but comparable minor bouts of illness'.

EWOs may have social work training though this is not required. They may be helped by voluntary school care workers, who support the work of the EWOs with schools and families. Even in authorities which provide an extensive education welfare service there may not be enough to go round. Another problem is that there may be overlap between the services provided by local authority social workers and the EWOs, which parents can find confusing.

Circular 2186, *School attendance and education welfare services*, supports the view that the main task of education welfare officers should be school attendance, and that other social problems should be passed on to the appropriate agencies.

Parents can find out from the school or the Education Office whether there is an EWO attached or linked to their school. It is not necessary to go through the school to contact the EWOs, they can be approached direct.

8 Who pays?

It was the 1944 Act that made secondary education available to all, and established the principle that 'no fees shall be charged in respect of admission to any school maintained by a local authority, . . . or in respect of the education provided in any such school'.

Forty years on, where have we got to? Even in 1944, it was recognised that parents might need extra help, even though tuition was free, to enable their children to benefit from the education provided for them. Section 81 of the 1944 Act gave the LEAs power to defray expenses for children attending county schools, voluntary schools and special schools so that they could 'take advantage without hardship to themselves or to their parents of any educational facilities available to them'.

Parents and children still need help, and there is no doubt that some suffer hardship which prevents them from benefitting from the education system. Many parents may not be aware of the grants and help that are available.

National and local finance for schools

The LEA pays for buildings, teachers and resources for its own schools and most of the running costs of voluntary schools. Education takes up at least half of most local authorities' spending, the most expensive item in the education budget being teachers' salaries. That is the main reason why teachers have to fight so hard for a pay increase. The money to pay for this spending comes from three sources: the rates, central government, and fees and charges. Fees and charges for meals, adult education courses, etc, make up a very small proportion – on average under 10% – of the total.

In recent years, the government's drive to cut public expenditure has had a double effect on education spending. Firstly, the proportion of spending subsidised out of central government funds, the Rate Support Grant, has dropped. In 1976 it was about 66%. The latest target for 1986–87 was around 47%. Secondly, the government, through the rate-capping legislation, has imposed limits on the income LEAs can raise from local rates.

The system is highly complex, and undergoing change. It depends basically on Grant Related Expenditure Assessment. GREA is a government attempt at measuring what a local authority 'needs' to spend on its various services to provide them at a standard level. The education Grant Related Expenditure (GRE) is decided by the Secretary of State for the Environment, based on material supplied by DES civil servants and LEA officers. It is not an absolute figure, calculated on what an LEA might ideally want or need to provide. Each LEA's GRE is a proportion of the total sum the government want to spend on education. That is why LEAs often complain that they cannot give a proper service on what the GRE would allow them.

At present (1986–87 budget), the GREs for all the different services are lumped together to give the total Rate Support Grant – one *block grant* – which local authorities can then allocate as they choose. Some LEAs do not allocate the whole amount designated as the education GRE to education, while others squeeze something out of one of the other budgets to give education a little more.

High-spending authorities who spend above their GRE receive less Rate Support Grant. Tony Travers, a Senior Research Fellow at the North East London Polytechnic, is one of the few people who understand how the Rate Support Grant system works. He does his best to explain it simply: 'If an Authority increases its spending over GRE, most Authorities will find that their block grant declines; if they spend more than five percent over GRE, grant will fall more quickly, while any reduction in spending will bring in more grant', (*Education* 2.8.85).

For the biggest spenders it does not stop there. They can no longer make up any shortfall in the block grant by increasing the local rates, because they are now subject to rate-capping. Rate-capped authorities may not levy a rate higher than that permitted by the Department of the Environment.

Education is bound to be affected by any cuts in public spending, because it takes up a significant proportion of the total. The last five years have seen a decline in real terms, taking into account inflation. Though the number of children has fallen, the demands on the service, particularly for adult education are rising all the time.

Education Support Grants

In 1984, the *Education (grants and awards) Act* gave the Secretary of State the power to make special grants to LEAs. These Education Support grants cover seventy percent of money spent on 'educational purposes' that the Secretary of State wants to encourage. Projects have to be approved in advance by the DES. According to the Regulations accompanying the Act, the purposes likely to be approved include, amongst others, teacher appraisal, teaching of maths and science, multi-cultural education, and information technology. For the 1986–87 budget, proposals could also be submitted on training for governors, help for parents of children under five with special needs, and combating drug abuse. About £40 million available for 1986–87.

Section 11 grants

The Home Office can make special grants to local authorities under Section 11 of the Local Government Act 1966. This allows the Home Office to pay seventy-five percent grants towards the cost of special provision, when 'a substantial number of immigrants from the Commonwealth whose language and customs differ from those of the local community', live in the area. The LEA applies direct to the Home Office for these grants, but if a school thinks it has a suitable project, it can submit it through the LEA.

LEA budgeting

An LEA's budget consists of two kinds of spending. Current expenditure consists of salaries and day-to-day running costs. Capital expenditure pays for land, buildings, and major equipment and furniture. LEAs usually make a distinction between major works – large capital projects, like a new building – and minor works – less expensive improvements. Repairs are not normally counted as capital expenditure. The government controls all local authority capital spending, as part of its public spending plans, and limits the amount of capital spending by each LEA.

Bearing in mind all the constraints, the LEA has to fix its annual budget according to its own priorities. It must find the money for the statutory services – enough schools for everyone of school age, and the other services it has a duty to provide. Even in the statutory provision, decisions about levels of staffing, and how much to spend on books, materials, equipment and maintenance, vary widely from one LEA to another. Then there are choices about how much to spend on nursery education, grants to voluntary bodies, adult education, recreation, etc. So within the controls the government imposes, there is scope for local decision-making.

To take just one example: in 1984, Bromley provided a nursery class or nursery school place for two percent of its children aged three or four. In Sutton, a similar London borough, the figure was fifteen percent. And in Sheffield, thirty-seven percent of children had a nursery place.

You can get some idea of how your LEA compares with others by looking at the statistics of the Chartered Institute of Public Finance and Accountancy, which give a detailed run-down on every aspect of LEA spending. They are obtainable from CIPFA, or any good reference library.

School allowances

Once the major decisions have been taken, the teachers and resources are allocated to the schools. Most of a school's allocation is decided according to the number and ages of the pupils. Extra staff and allowances may be available for particular needs. Schools may get extra cash for a building that is difficult to run, or if they have buildings on several sites. Some LEAs have an index of educational priority, which is calculated according to the social and economic background of the pupils. Schools get extra resources according to their place on the index.

As well as the school allowance, also known as capitation, there are special funds a school may be able to draw on. There may be a school travel grant, which can be used to subsidise school journeys. The LEA may make special grants available to encourage new developments in the curriculum, for example, computer education. LEA-wide services, like the Education Welfare Service, are funded centrally and are not charged to the schools.

Any capital spending a school is allowed comes out of a different budget. Full-scale re-decoration and other maintenance would be paid for centrally; the money for small improvements and repairs might have to be found from the school allowance.

To sum up, county schools will not have to worry about finding the money for the buildings and furniture, or to pay teachers and non-teaching staff. The capitation allowance will be used mainly to provide books and materials for the various departments, and the facilities that are used by everyone, such as the photocopier, or audio-visual equipment. Depending on the LEA, it may also cover exam entrance fees, telephone and fuel bills, and items like the use of school buses for outings.

Voluntary schools get the same staffing and capitation allowances from the LEA as county schools, but they have to pay towards the cost of their buildings, (except for controlled schools who get all their building costs from the LEA). Voluntary aided and special agreement schools have to find 15% of their building, external repair and improvement costs themselves. They receive the remaining 85% as a grant from the DES. The LEA pays for internal maintenance. 15% may not sound much, but it can be a burden to schools, especially if they do not have their own endowments.

How do schools spend their money?

The decisions about how the school allowance should be spent are made by the head, who has to arbitrate between the claims of the different departments, some of whom have much higher running costs than others. A helpful account of this process is given by Rick Rogers in the ACE Information sheet, *The school budget – your business*.

Some LEAs still provide the allowance under separate headings – so much for books, so much for materials, etc. Unless the head has *virement*, which is the power to switch spending from one heading to another, so that less can be spent on books, and more on computers, for instance, the scope for laying out the money effectively can be limited.

Governors may be asked to approve the school budget, though this has often been a formality. Now that governors take their responsibilities more seriously, they expect to be involved in the policies that underlie the budget decisions. The school often expects parents and governors to support their requests to the LEA for more resources. They are more likely to do this when they are kept fully informed about the needs and limitations of the existing budget.

Financial independence for schools

LEAs are beginning to accept the idea that when you give schools more financial responsibility, the money spent on education is used more effectively. To take a very simple example, 'phone bills can fall dramatically when the school has to pay the bill out of its allowance, instead of sending it up to County Hall. Some LEAs give schools an extra allowance which can be spent on 'buying' teaching and non-teaching staff hours as well as books and materials. Because schools almost always choose to spend most of the extra cash on staff, most LEAs find they have to set a limit on the proportion the school can use for staff. Otherwise the LEA can run into difficulties over tax and employment regulations.

Some LEAs have gone further than this, and are developing schemes for giving their schools a budget to cover all their costs, which they have to administer for themselves. Cambridgeshire set up a pilot scheme that gave the schools taking part the responsibility for:

- teaching staff (within certain limits);
- supply teachers for occasional absences of staff;
- all non-teaching staff except school-meals staff and groundsmen;
- rent and rates;
- fuel, light, water, cleaning materials, laundry, protective clothing;
- furniture and fittings;
- textbooks, library books, stationery and materials;
- exam fees;
- administrative, educational and domestic equipment;
- printing, office stationery, postage and telephones;
- educational visits, staff travelling and subsistence;
- income.

Heads found that the extra work involved was less than they had expected, and was compensated for to a greater extent because they no longer had to spend hours on the telephone to persuade the Office to give them what they needed. Officers, on the other hand, found that their work increased, though when people get used to the scheme, this may change.

All those concerned felt that the scheme had led to a better knowledge of the way the financial system operates, and heads reported that the staff and governors had a better understanding of the way in which educational and financial decisions are intertwined.

Any scheme for giving a school more control over its own budget can founder if schools are expected to take on the extra responsibilities without being given an equivalent increase in their allowances. Also, it seems only fair that schools should get the benefit of any savings made, so what is in it for the LEA, especially if extra officer time is needed to run the scheme? The answer is committed parents, staff and governors who understand more fully the difficulties the schools and the LEA are trying to overcome.

School fund

Most schools have a school fund, which consists of money raised by school activities such as the Christmas Bazaar, and the school photo and by donations from parents, etc. Children may be asked to bring so much a week for the fund. This is acceptable as long as no children are made to feel inferior because their parents do not contribute.

The head has control of these voluntary funds, and the LEA has no say in how they are spent. However, LEAs may, as employers, make regulations about how the accounts are kept and audited, and some Articles of Government require the head to present the accounts to the governors once a year.

School funds are a form of trust fund, and if money has been raised for a specific named object, such as a swimming pool, it must be spent on that. Otherwise the only limitation is that it should be spent for activities which benefit the children in the school. It is often helpful for the head to have a fund to draw on which can be used to help individual cases of hardship at short notice. Equipment for school plays and music, a strip for the school team, or playground equipment are other uses.

The school fund is, or should be, quite separate from any school association or PTA funds and should be kept in a different account. The head and the governors have no control over how school association funds are spent, though the head would usually be invited to make suggestions about items the school needs that the association could buy.

Grants

Various grants are available to help parents with the extra costs of educating their children. Some of these are mandatory, which means that the LEA has no choice about providing them, and must pay them according to a national scale. Others are discretionary, which means that the LEA can choose whether to provide them or not, and if they do decide to offer them, can also decide how much to pay and to whom.

How to apply

The information regulations (see page 12) say that LEAs must inform parents about the help given with transport, clothing, and milk and meals. It must also explain how to apply for these. Or, as the regulations put it 'the address from which parents may obtain detailed information as to the assistance in this regard which is available and eligibility therefor'. So you should be able to get all the information you need from the Education Offices. The school or the education welfare officer should be able to give help and advice.

The school, EWO or Education Office will send you details of how to apply. You do not necessarily have to apply through the school. Application forms are less complex and incomprehensible than they used to be, but they are still difficult to follow unless you are used to the jargon. The education welfare officer, or a local Citizen's Advice Bureau, or law centre are a source of help. Most grants are paid on a means-tested scale, and you will need to produce evidence of your income – recent pay slips, rent books, UB40s, etc. The amount you get will depend on your net income – what's left after mortgage/rent/rates, pension payments, fares to work, other family earnings, deductions for other dependent children, etc, and on the generosity of your LEA.

Fees and charges

According to Section 61 of the 1944 Act, the education service is free, so to what extent can parents be expected to pay for the services provided by an LEA? The answer is that if a subject is on the timetable, and part of the curriculum, it cannot be charged for.

This was established in a case brought against Hereford and Worcester LEA in 1981. The LEA had decided to make a charge for individual music tuition provided in their schools. The court ruled that this was illegal. Mr Justice Forbes spelt out the principles a) that playing an instrument was a perfectly proper component of education, and that it was reasonable for a school to have it as part of the curriculum; b) that if it was part of the curriculum, Section 61 applied, so that no fees could be charged for it.

However, there was a sting in the tail of the judgement, which LEAs did not hesitate to use. Mr Justice Forbes said that while it was reasonable to include music, there was no obligation on an LEA to do so. It was their prerogative to decide. Hereford and Worcester, and several other LEAs who charged for it, immediately decided to give up offering any music tuition at all. Other subjects, like swimming, for which charges had been made were also affected. The outcry was such that in Hereford and Worcester an uneasy compromise was reached. Generally, it is now agreed that LEAs can make a charge but only if the subject is offered outside school hours, and not timetabled. Teaching music as an exam subject is not affected, because that is clearly part of the timetable, nor is there any objection to an LEA offering free individual tuition if it wishes to do so.

Books and materials

It did not need the Hereford and Worcester judgement to prove that schools could not charge for essential books and stationery that were used in subjects on the timetable. It is of course up to the LEA and the school to decide just how many books and materials are needed.

Difficulties occur when it comes to practical subjects which have an end-product that children can take home; the apple crumble, cookery apron, or book-ends, for example. It is probably not illegal to make a charge for the cost of these. However, this does mean that children from poor families may not be able to afford to take subjects like Home Economics, or Craft, Design and Technology. Some Home Economics syllabuses expect pupils to have experience in cooking some rather expensive dishes, for which a poor scholar would have great difficulty in finding the cash. It has often been the case that practical subjects have not carried much clout in the discussions over the allocation of the school budget, so they have been underfunded, as compared with a prestigious academic subject, such as Physics.

This is something that parents should bring to the attention of the governors if it seems to be a problem in their school.

School outings

Strictly speaking, if an outing is in school time, and has an educational purpose, no charge should be made. But however generous an LEA may be in providing subsidies for school travel and outings, it is unlikely that a school can afford to pay all the cost of every trip. And most school outings are part education, part holiday. So unless parents are willing to make a contribution, not many visits can take place. It is, however, unacceptable for children to be left behind because their parents cannot or will not afford to pay. The school fund, or the education welfare service, may be able to help.

Travel to school

LEAs must arrange for free travel to and from school for children who live more than walking distance away. Walking distance is defined as more than three miles for children over eight years old, and two miles for children under eight, by the nearest available route. This distance is very carefully measured, and has been the subject of several court cases. In Shaxted v Ward in 1954, it was held that the fact that the parents thought part of it was unsafe was immaterial. An earlier case had decided that the 'route' could include a cart track that was an approach to the child's home.

However, a case in 1985 (which may go to appeal) changed the commonly held view that the safety of a particular route did not matter. In Rogers v Essex County Council, the judge ruled in favour of the parent who claimed that no responsible parent would allow a child to walk alone through a lonely area known as Copford Plains, and that it was hardly safe even for a mother and child. He said: 'To regard Parliament as having intended that there should be regarded as an available route something, such as a public footpath, which was dangerous even for adults, and which was so dangerous for children that no responsible parent would allow a child of the relevant age to use it, is in my view, to impute to Parliament an unacceptable disregard for the safety of children'. This decision, if it stands, could cause considerable problems for LEAs in deciding who should get free travel.

When a dividing line is drawn on the basis of distance, it is bound to cause some hard cases. For example, near the boundary line it is quite possible for some children to get free passes while others using the same bus-stop are not eligible because they live a hundred yards or so nearer the school.

It is difficult to offer a choice of schools to parents, without at the same time making it feasible for their children to be able to attend any school of their choice within reasonable distance.

Various attempts to rationalise, and reduce the cost of school transport have failed because it seems to be impossible to create a fairer system without causing hardship to parents.

Free travel may be provided either by supplying travel passes to the qualifying children, or by arranging for school buses to collect and deliver them. Where only a few children are involved and there is no suitable public transport, taxis may be used.

Concessionary fares may be provided for children even if they do not live outside the statutory distance. Some LEAs provide free travel for children who live near the boundary, or who have a particularly dangerous journey on foot. LEAs can offer spare seats on school buses or taxis to fare-paying passengers, including children living nearer the school, at a reasonable cost. LEAs can arrange with the local transport authority to provide 'half-passes' so that pupils over sixteen, who live inside the statutory distance, can get half fares travelling to and from school.

CHILDREN WITH SPECIAL NEEDS

When children are unable to travel to school on public transport, most LEAs will provide transport for them, whatever distance they live from school. This may be on specially adapted buses, with helpers who travel with the children to assist them on and off the bus and ensure their safety.

BOARDING SCHOOL

If children are at boarding school because no suitable school is available for them near their home, the LEA must pay the fares to and from school at the beginning and end of term, and at half term. If the school closes at other times, the LEA must pay the fares home and back. Some LEAs will also pay for occasional visits home during term-time, and for parents who cannot afford it otherwise to visit their child during term, if this is thought to be beneficial for the child.

Milk and meals

The 1980 Act did away with the LEA's duty to provide school meals, of a nutritional standard laid down by the DES, to all the pupils who wanted them. Instead, LEAs now have the power to provide such meals and refreshment as they think fit, and to make what charges they wish for these.

They must still provide some kind of midday meal free-of-charge for children whose parents are on supplementary benefit or receive Family Income Supplement. This no longer has to be 'suitable in all respects as the main meal of the day'. The LEA must take advice on what would be appropriate, according to local needs. Circular 1/80 which describes the effect of the changes made by the Act, says that 'in general, the kind of meal that is available to pupils who pay will be appropriate'.

LEAs must also provide, free-of-charge, facilities for children to eat a packed lunch they have brought from home. This will include accommodation, furniture and supervision to enable pupils to eat 'in a civilised manner'. It would not include cooking facilities.

LEAs are given a duty to consider whether other children need free meals and milk, perhaps those with difficult family circumstances who are not on social security. A number of LEAs use their powers to subsidise meals and give free meals on a more generous scale than the Act requires, but it was suggested in the 1985 Green paper on social security that this power to subsidise meals should be removed, and that children whose parents receive Family Income Supplement should no longer be eligible for free meals. Many nutritionists fear that this would have serious consequences for the general standard of child health.

LEAs can get a subsidy from the EEC to serve cheap or free milk in schools. Most LEAs provide free milk for children with special needs and for those who get free school meals. Some offer it free to other age groups. Some LEAs will only provide milk, with the EEC subsidy, at a price that covers all their costs.

Many LEAs have changed over to a cash cafeteria system for milk, meals and other refreshments, in an effort to cut costs, and make school meals more popular. The difficulty is that although the cafeterias try to offer a balanced diet, children tend to want chips with everything. If chips are not on the menu, the children go elsewhere for their food. Schools which make an effort to teach their pupils about healthy diets as part of their health education syllabus seem to be better at persuading children to eat sensibly at school.

Circular 1/80 asks LEAs to ensure that as far as possible arrangements made for children taking free meals are 'such as will minimise identification and possible embarrassment'. So if a school is causing distress to children on free dinners, parents should draw their attention to the Circular and ask for a more sensitive system to be adopted.

NON-MAINTAINED SCHOOLS

The same provisions about milk and meals apply to non-maintained special schools. They must provide meals for pupils on supplementary benefit, or receiving Family Income Supplement. They must make facilities available to pupils bringing their own food. They can make a reasonable charge for any meals supplied to other children.

There are no longer any regulations about the quality of food to be supplied to children in non-maintained special boarding schools. The DES takes the view that schools will not be approved unless they provide satisfactory standards. It requires the school to keep records of the food served so that anyone inspecting the record would be able to judge whether the diet is satisfactory. The governing body ought therefore to keep an eye on the quality of the food provided, and ask to see the records regularly.

Clothing grants

LEAs have the power to make three kinds of clothing grant. These are all discretionary, and the amounts given vary widely from one LEA to another.

UNIFORM GRANTS

Uniform grants can be given to any pupils both at maintained schools and at non-maintained schools. The fact that a school insists on a uniform does not mean that the LEA will necessarily pay a uniform grant, even to the poorest families. (If a child has an assisted place at an independent school, there is a national scale for paying uniform grants (see page 152).) Some LEAs will make grants although no distinctive clothing is required by the school. LEAs that do make grants often use the same means tests and scales as they apply for free school meals. Some make grants at regular intervals, to keep up with children's growth rates, others pay a once-and-for-all grant when the child starts secondary school.

NECESSITOUS CLOTHING GRANTS

Necessitous clothing grants can be made by LEAs to children whose clothing is so inadequate or unsuitable that they cannot take advantage of the education they are receiving. LEAs can provide suitable clothing, and make a charge for it to the parents if they believe that the parents could afford to pay. LEAs can also do this for children at independent schools, though as far as possible this should not cost more than it would if the child was at a maintained school. Necessitous clothing grants are often paid in the form of vouchers which can be used only at certain shops. This can cause distress and embarrassment to parents, and may not always be the most economical way to buy clothes.

PE AND GAMES KIT

PE and games kit may be provided for individuals, or a stock may be provided for general use in a school. When LEAs provide clothing, this may either be lent or given to the child. If the child becomes the sole owner, parents may be required to pay towards the cost.

Clubs, societies, outings and school journeys

LEAs can provide help with all these extra-curricular activities if they choose to do so. If an LEA grant is not available, the school may have access to other money, from the school fund or School Association, to help children who might otherwise be barred from these activities through lack of cash.

School journeys are very popular, and can give children valuable experience through communal living away from home, quite apart from any specific educational purpose for the trip. However, parents sometimes feel that the school journeys arranged by their school are expensive, and have little educational value. They can ask the governors to investigate the school's policy, and especially to enquire what arrangements are made for children who stay behind.

As well as subsidising the overall cost through a school journey fund, and helping individuals who cannot afford to pay, LEAs can make other facilities available. They may, for example, run their own field centres and hostels, which are cheaper than those run by outside organisations.

Special talents

LEAs can decide to make discretionary grants to pupils with unusual talent in music, dance or drama, so that they can attend fee-paying schools which provide special tuition. The LEA will usually impose strict conditions on the payment of such grants, and will often only pay for pupils who have been accepted at well-established schools.

In addition to LEA grants, the Secretary of State, under the powers given in Section 100 of the 1944 Act, has designated a few schools to take part in an aided pupil scheme for music and ballet schools. The *Education (grants), (music and ballet schools), regulations 1985* name five schools: Chetham's School of Music in Manchester, the Purcell School in Harrow, the Royal Ballet School, the Wells Cathedral School in Somerset, and the Yehudi Menuhin School.

The regulations give these schools the right to offer aided places to suitably qualified pupils. The schools receive a grant from the DES for the money spent on the scheme. Pupils get a grant towards the cost of fees, board and lodging in a boarding school, uniform and travel to and from school. This is given according to a scale laid down by the DES, on similar lines to the Assisted Places Scheme.

Educational maintenance allowances for pupils over 16

LEAs can make grants to encourage children to stay on at school after they are sixteen. However, very few LEAs do this, and the amounts paid are not large, around £7 a week from the more generous LEAs. The grants are usually made on the same scale as free school meals.

People over sixteen who stay on at school or in full-time education at college are not eligible to claim social security in their own right, unless they are disabled, or orphans, or looking after their own children. They may also be able to claim if they can prove that they are living away from home, have no contact with their parents and are not given any support by them.

The DHSS twenty-one hours rule applies to people over sixteen who have left school and want to study part-time. This means that people who take a course involving not more than twenty-one hours' study can claim social security. The rules are difficult to follow, but the college should be able to advise students on which of their courses are acceptable.

Independent school fees

LEAs have the power to make grants towards the cost of fees at independent schools. They may not pay for children with a statement of special educational needs to attend an independent school unless it has been approved by the Secretary of State. There are no other limitations on the LEA's powers, but a number of authorities will pay school fees only in special cases. LEAs in more prosperous middle-class areas are most likely to have a generous policy on paying school fees.

There is wide variation too in the extent to which LEAs are prepared to subsidise other costs of independent education, such as uniform, travel, examination fees, and school trips and journeys, also the cost of tuition for extras like music, or additional teaching. They are more sympathetic to these extras when they are subsidising places for children with special needs.

Assisted Places Scheme

LEAs cut back the number of places at independent schools that they were prepared to subsidise places when the Assisted Places Scheme was introduced. This was set up under the 1980 Act, and is a national scheme under which the DES make a participatory agreement with independent schools who wish to join the scheme. The DES reimburses the participating schools for the costs of subsidising places for pupils who might not otherwise 'be able to benefit from education at independent schools'.

The *Education (assisted places) regulations 1985* set out the rules for the scheme. Schools select their own pupils, the only stipulations being that they must be over eleven and either have lived in the United Kingdom for the last two years, or have some other residence qualification. Children with refugee status may also be considered. When the scheme began, LEAs could veto the transfer of a pupil from a maintained school into the sixth-form of an independent school. Under the 1985 regulations, LEAs have no right of veto. At least 60% of the children with assisted places in a school must have previously been educated in a maintained school. However, the *Education (assisted places) (incidental expenses) regulations 1981* require the schools to pay means-tested allowances towards incidental expenses, including school uniform, travel to and from school if the home is more than three miles away, meals and charges for field trips. Schools are reimbursed for the costs of these allowances by the DES.

Schools offering assisted places have to publish details of the number of places available, and the way in which pupils are selected for them, together with other details about the school.

Parents have to give the schools full information about their income and outgoings. The proportion of the fees parents have to pay depends on their net income after allowances have been made for other dependents, mortgage, etc. Parents with a net income of £6,376 pay nothing; parents with a net income of £12,280 pay the whole cost.

In 1985, approximately 18,000 children were taking part in the scheme, at over two hundred schools. About 70% had come from maintained schools. The scheme was costing the DES £22.5 million.

Help for Service families

Service families who are paying boarding school fees are entitled in certain circumstances to the Ministry of Defence Boarding School Allowance. This is to enable Service families to ensure the continuity of their children's education. The allowance does not cover the whole cost of tuition and boarding expenses, and Service families can also apply for LEA assistance with independent school fees. Any Boarding School Allowance is taken into account when calculating their income.

Other sources of help

If the LEA is not prepared to help with independent school fees, and parents have to pay themselves, there are schemes for spreading the burden of the cost. You can get advice on this from ISIS, or from the charitable trusts like Gabbitas Thring or Truman and Knightley, which exist to provide free advice to parents about schooling. Grandparents can make covenants, for example, that enable parents to reclaim tax from the Inland Revenue.

Many large firms will help senior staff by paying school fees for their children, which is a valuable perk.

Student grants

Students who are taking a degree level or similar approved course are eligible for mandatory grants from their LEA. These cover all college dues and tuition fees, plus a means-tested maintenance allowance towards the cost of board and lodging, travel, books, and pocket money. Parents are expected to pay a contribution towards this on the basis of their income. Disabled students may be able to claim extra allowances if their disability hinders their studies. The National Bureau for Handicapped Students can give advice on this.

LEAs can also make discretionary grants to students who are not taking degree level courses, but these tend to be less generous than the mandatory grants and LEAs cut back on them when resources are limited.

The DES booklet *Grants to students: a brief guide*, available free from DES Publications, gives all the details about degree level grants. You can find out about discretionary grants to students from the local Education Offices.

If parents pay their contribution towards maintenance by covenant, tax at 30% can be reclaimed from the Inland Revenue. The National Union of Students publishes a leaflet *Covenants for Students* explaining how to do this.

Trust funds

LEAs often administer a number of local educational trusts, which can be used to make grants in cases of hardship. Other local charitable trusts can offer grants for educational purposes. Some of these are on a small scale, and because of the rules laid down by the founder, occasionally have difficulty in finding suitable candidates for grants. The education welfare officer should know about local sources of this kind. National charities may also be able to help in special cases, particularly when children have special needs. The Charities Aid Foundation publish a *Directory of grant-making trusts*, which should be in a central reference library. Most charities have thousands of applications for help, so you need to present a good case, and apply well in advance.

9

Who does what and how to get things changed

The Department of Education and Science

At the top of the educational pyramid is the Secretary of State for Education and Science, a politician with a seat in the Cabinet, who leads the Department of Education and Science (DES). The DES is responsible for government policy on schools, colleges, further, higher and adult education, science, and the supply and training of teachers.

The Secretary of State is assisted by a Minister of State, who is given responsibility for teaching quality, education 16–19, TVEI (Technical and Vocational Education Initiative see page 31), relations with MSC, etc. There are two parliamentary under secretaries, also politicians. One looks after higher education, science, continuing education and the Open University, the other deals mainly with schools and LEA matters, governing bodies and the youth service.

The Secretary of State for Wales and the Welsh Office are responsible for Welsh primary, secondary and further education, along with the supply of teachers in Wales. In practice, many circulars and regulations are issued jointly by the DES and the Welsh Office, though the Welsh Office put out circulars on specifically Welsh affairs such as the teaching of Welsh in schools.

The Scottish education system is entirely separate, and is the responsibility of the Secretary of State for Scotland and the Scottish Education Department.

In Northern Ireland, education is the responsibility of the Northern Ireland Secretary and the Northern Ireland Department of Education, and is provided locally by the Education and Library Boards.

What powers does the DES have over what goes on in schools?

'A national service locally administered'; this is the classic description of the way in which the education service is organised, but what does it mean in practice? The 1944 Act gave the Secretary of State the duty to promote the education of the people of England and Wales, and to 'secure the effective execution by local authorities, under his control and direction, of the national policy for providing a varied and comprehensive education service in every area'.

However, because the Act gave LEAs the job of providing education in their areas, this control and direction is limited. In simple terms, the DES must see that LEAs are providing sufficient and suitable education but cannot direct them how to provide it except where a legal right to do this is given in the education acts. For example, the Secretary of State can issue regulations, which are statutory instruments and have the force of law, so LEAs and schools must keep to them. But these regulations can only be issued when a specific power to do so has been included in the relevant education act.

The DES can also put out circulars, circular letters and memoranda which offer advice and explain government policy. Although schools and LEAs would be expected to take note of these, they are not legally enforceable. A court judgement in 1980 (R v ILEA ex parte Bradby) made this clear. It said that ignoring the advice given in a circular might well be contributory evidence that an LEA was acting unreasonably, though that would depend on the facts of the case. But LEAs did not have to comply with the circular which was 'no more than advice and guidance from the Minister as to a course, which in general, he suggests the education authority should follow'. (Regulations and circulars can be obtained from DES Publications.)

The DES can ask Her Majesty's Inspectorate (see page 163) to look at and report on subjects in which the Department is particularly interested. The hope is that when the HMIs publicise what they regard as good practice, and draw attention to bad practice, this will influence what is going on in the schools.

Finally, as explained in **A say in school staffing,** page 82, the DES can use the power of the purse to persuade LEAs to do what the government wants. The Department also determines how many teachers should be trained and what qualifications they should have (see page 86).

DES statistics

The DES collects statistics about educational provision throughout the country, and publishes a series of statistical bulletins on various subjects, for example, pupil–teacher ratios for each LEA, numbers of schools and pupils, children under five in school. These are obtainable free from the DES. They provide much useful information, and can be helpful in finding out how your LEA compares with other authorities.

The DES as court of appeal

The DES does have the power to intervene on some matters that are of great importance to parents. Although the DES seldom rules in favour of parents in dispute with a school or an LEA, this does not mean that its powers are of no value to parents. They are often more effective as a threat because schools or LEAs do not like having their actions, and the reasons for them, exposed to the investigation of the Department, with the possibility of bad publicity to follow.

Section 68 of the 1944 Act gave the Secretary of State the power to intervene to prevent an LEA or a school from acting unreasonably. This applies even when the authority has the legal power to take the disputed decision.

It used to be thought that once the Secretary of State was satisfied that the proposed action was unreasonable, the ruling made could not be challenged. But the Tameside case in 1977 changed that interpretation of the law. The judge said that the facts on which the Secretary of State made the decision could be challenged, and if they were found to be incorrect the ruling itself might also be wrong.

The Tameside case was also significant because it set out the law's view of what 'reasonable' meant. It was a very strict interpretation. 'Unreasonable' conduct was conduct that no sensible authority, acting with due appreciation of its responsibilities, could have decided to adopt. In other words, you have to be able to show that no sensible person would have behaved in that particular way.

Another important point about Section 68 is that if you are objecting to an unreasonable exercise of authority, you must complain to the Secretary of State first, you cannot go direct to the courts. But if you are claiming that the authority has acted *ultra vires* – acted in a way that it did not have the legal power to do – or has behaved contrary to natural justice, then you can go to the courts first, without appealing to the Secretary of State.

Section 99 gives the Secretary of State the power to intervene if an LEA or a school is failing to fulfil its duties under the education acts. If satisfied that a complaint is justified, the Secretary of State can order the authority to rectify the failure. Unfortunately, it has been difficult to persuade the Secretary of State to act. Parents have tried, for example, to obtain a ruling that an LEA was not providing adequate resources in its schools. The Secretary of State has refused to intervene on the grounds that standards of provision vary widely and it is therefore difficult to prove that resources are inadequate.

Parents did win one battle over Section 99. Haringey parents, fed up with their schools being closed because of a strike of caretakers, asked the Secretary of State to direct the LEA to open the schools. The request was refused, so the parents went to court to ask for a writ to compel the schools to open, quoting Section 8 of the 1944 Act which said that the LEA had a duty to provide education. The schools re-opened before the case could be heard, but the parents obtained a ruling that they had the right to apply to the courts because they were claiming that the LEA was *ultra vires* in supporting the strike.

Sections 12 and 13 of the 1980 Act give the Secretary of State the right to make the final decision over whether a school should be closed or significantly changed in character, if local people disagree with the proposals.

Local education authorities

Local education authorities (LEAs) are the direct providers of schools and colleges, and they have a duty to make sure that efficient education, throughout the three stages of primary, secondary and further education, is available to meet the needs of the population in their area.

There are 104 education authorities in England and Wales. In the shire counties, the eight Welsh counties and the metropolitian districts, the county council or the metropolitan district council is the local education authority. In London, the twenty outer London boroughs are LEAs and the twelve Inner London boroughs, plus the City of London, make up the Inner London Education Authority (ILEA). Each local education authority must have an Education Committee, with membership drawn from the elected councillors, and co-opted members having a special interest in education. These may include parents, teachers, representatives of the churches and local industry. The ILEA has always been a special case, and in 1986 becomes even more unusual, because it will consist of members directly elected to serve only on the education authority.

Education Committees set up sub-committees to deal with various aspects of their work, the most relevant for parents usually being the Schools sub-committee. The membership of all the committees will reflect the balance of political power of the Council itself. Even co-options will normally be done on a party political basis, and if there is a majority party on the council it will make sure that its nominees chair all the sub-committees. Except in Inner London, the main council can overrule the Education Committee's decisions if it chooses to do so. In any case, the political parties will normally have held caucus meetings beforehand and instructed their members on how to vote on any controversial issue.

Meetings and minutes of the Education Committee, and most of its sub-committees, are open to the public, unless it has been decided to meet in private on a particular issue. Anyone interested in local educational issues will find it worthwhile to subscribe to the agendas and minutes on a regular basis, in order to keep an eye on what is going on.

Staff

The Education Committee must appoint a Chief Education Officer, sometimes called Director of Education or some similar title. He, (sad to say very few women have ever been appointed, and there are none at the time of writing), will be in charge of a staff of education officers and deputies in charge of different sections of the service. All senior staff have normally had some teaching experience. Other staff are local government officers who may work permanently in education or transfer to other local authority departments. Many officers are deeply committed to the education service, and can prove valuable allies to members of the public who are campaigning for improvements. They can be useful in resolving problems, and it is always worth enlisting their help and support.

It is helpful to understand the structure of the local service, and to know which councillors serve on which committees and which staff have responsibility for the various sections. Normally, this information is available on demand from the LEA. If not, you may need the help of a friendly councillor to find out. Some of the information will be listed in the *Education yearbook*.

You can find out the address and telephone number of your local Education Offices from the town hall or local telephone book.

What powers do LEAs have over what goes on in schools?

LEAs make most of the crucial local decisions on schools, staffing, and resources. The best way to influence these is to convince your local councillors that you have a good case, and that it is politically expedient to listen to you.

This is particularly important in the areas where the LEA has the power to provide a service, but no legal duty to do so. The distinction is between what is mandatory – the LEA must, for example, see that there are enough school places for all the children of statutory school age – and discretionary – the LEA is expected to provide an adult education service but does not have to ensure that there is a place for everyone who wants to study Italian at evening-class.

LEAs also decide the general educational policies for their area – how children should be admitted to county schools, appointments procedures, school meals, etc. They may also lay down policy guidelines on such matters as children with special needs in the ordinary school, equal opportunities, discipline in schools, and can influence the curriculum through their inspectorate or advisory service (see page 162).

A good example of how the LEA can influence what is taught in schools is the ILEA SMILE project. In order to improve the standard of maths teaching and learning, the Authority developed new materials, syllabuses and methods of teaching. Teachers were offered in-service training on the project, and the inspectors encouraged schools to take it up. Many ILEA schools now use the SMILE system enthusiastically, but no school could be forced to adopt it if they do not wish to do so.

You must understand that traditionally, LEAs are very reluctant to interfere in matters that come under the heading of internal management and discipline in the school, unless you can show that the LEA's own regulations and policies are being infringed. As long as the head and governors are keeping within the LEA guidelines, it is very unlikely that the LEA will overturn their decisions about the way the school is run.

Who are the inspectors and what do they do?

LEA inspectors are almost always qualified teachers, with wide experience in their subject and in education generally. Very often, they are former heads of schools. They are known as advisers in many LEAs.

There are no regulations about how many inspectors an LEA should employ. Some have a well-developed system of district general inspectors supported by specialist inspectors for different areas of the curriculum. Others may not. You can find out how many inspectors your LEA employs from the *Education yearbook*, which lists their names and responsibilities for each LEA.

LEA inspectors provide advice on the curriculum, teaching methods, new buildings and equipment. They communicate the LEA's general policy to the schools, and encourage schools to carry out any special policy initiatives. They also relay what is going on in schools and the concerns of the head and staff back to the LEA.

For example, suppose an LEA was worried about the level of maths teaching in its schools. It could call on the maths inspectorate to collect information about effective teaching methods and materials, from its local schools and elsewhere, and look at recent research and development and any relevant HMI reports. The inspectors could then make this material accessible to schools, could advise individual teachers, and would probably run in-service courses which all maths teachers would be invited to attend free of charge.

LEA inspectors are responsible for probationary teachers, and for deciding in consultation with the school whether or not they are performing satisfactorily. They will advise the LEA and the schools on staffing. It is usually the inspector who can arrange for a school to have extra resources for a particular subject, extra teachers, full or part-time, and extra Burnham points for scale posts. The inspectorate is often involved in the assessment of children with special needs, particularly in deciding whether a child can attend an ordinary school and in helping the school to accommodate children with special educational needs.

Inspectors play an important part in the assessment of all teachers, not just probationers. They will normally be responsible for the appraisal of the performance of all the teachers employed in the area, and may write their references when they are applying for a new job.

In some areas it is the inspector who interviews and appoints new staff. When governors are responsible for interviewing, an inspector will normally be present to give professional advice.

So altogether inspectors can exert a powerful influence over the education provided in an LEA. Parents do not have any direct access to the inspectorate, though there is nothing to stop a parent writing to an inspector if they wish to bring something to their attention. Governors should make an effort to get to know their local inspector well; a start could be made by asking the inspector to come and speak at a governor's meeting.

Her Majesty's Inspectorate (HMI)

Her Majesty's Inspectors are appointed by the Crown in order to emphasise their independence from the government, the LEAs and the schools. There are 490 HMIs in England and Wales, with a head office at the DES under a Senior Chief Inspector, and regional offices covering the whole of England and Wales. HMIs usually become inspectors around the age of thirty-five, on the basis of their experience as teachers and lecturers and their specialist knowledge. Most HMIs are responsible for a group of schools, and a specialist area of education.

Their job is to monitor the overall standard of education, to compare and contrast institutions, to spread ideas about the curriculum and teaching methods, and to assess the quality of teaching generally, though they do not report on individual teachers.

Every year they do a few formal inspections of schools and colleges, and an overall assessment of the provision in one or two LEAs. The reports on these full inspections are published and are available to the public, from the LEA, the school, or the DES Publications Despatch Centre.

A DES leaflet for parents about HMI, *HM Inspectors today: standards in education* described their method of work as follows: 'They offer the best professional judgements they can about what they see when they visit education institutions, administrative offices or professional bodies and institutions. They have no powers. They have to earn attention by what they are and what they do . . . . Perhaps their most significant characteristics are their professional independence . . . and their obligation to report as they find without fear or favour.'

Some idea of the scope of their activity can be gained from a look at the entries for HMI in the index of the magazine *Education* for the last half of 1984:

Curriculum matters: Welsh;
Damning report on Haringey;
Day release in Wales criticised;
Education Observed (a review of published reports);
Follow-up report on North London Polytechnic;
Haringey report politically motivated allegation;
Hereford and Worcester chief complains to Sir Keith about report;
Major building defects in Redbridge;
Mother tongue teaching in school and community (a report);
Muslim school criticised;
NUT leaps to the defence of HMI independence;
Norfolk's shortcomings and the LEA response;
Practical and emotional responses to an inspection;
Report critical of Craft Design and Technology teaching;
Report criticises Muslim girls' high school in Dewsbury;
Report on field trips;
Report on slow learners in secondary schools;
Report on traveller children in West Sussex;
Reports on army schools;
Survey on the Youth Training Scheme in further education;
Unenthusiastic over Workers' Education Association courses for the unemployed;
Report on computer studies;
Welsh Office response to report on under achievers.

Parents who want to contact HMIs can write to their regional offices or to the Senior Chief Inspector, c/o the DES. HMIs are not likely to take up an individual complaint about a school, but may respond to matters of general concern about the education provided in an LEA.

The school

Every school has a governing body, now that the 1980 Education Act has been fully implemented, and every school has an Instrument and Articles of Government. These are legal documents, drawn up by the LEA in county schools, and by the foundation in voluntary schools. The DES has to approve all voluntary school Instruments and Articles, and those for county secondary schools.

The Instrument explains who should be governors of the school, how they are appointed, and how governors' meetings are organised. The Articles set out the way in which powers are distributed between the head, the governing body and the LEA. Normally, the LEA decides the general educational character of the school and its place in the local school system, the governors are given the general direction of the conduct and curriculum, and the head is given responsibility for the internal organisation, management and discipline of the school.

The power of the head

It should be clear from reading this handbook that in most of the matters that concern parents, the person with the immediate responsibility is the head of the school. The absolute power they once had has been subtly diminished in various ways. They have to take account, more than they did in the past, of the many constraints, checks and balances inside and outside the school, and they will certainly have to carry their staff, governors and parents with them if they wish to make significant changes in school policy. But their individual skills of leadership and decision-making are fundamental to the quality of their school.

Heads of county schools are subject to regulations made by the LEA and as employees are expected to carry out the LEA's educational policies.

Heads of voluntary schools are not subject to LEA regulations or policies, unless the Articles of Government provide for this. They are employed by the governors.

The basis of the head's power to determine how a school is to be conducted lies in the responsibility given to heads for the internal management of the school. As long as they are not breaching any regulations or policies that the LEA or the DES may legally enforce, heads have the final say in decisions about organisation, school and discipline. There is always the sanction of reasonableness, and there are, of course, some matters where the Articles give a right of appeal to the governors, or where the LEA has kept the final responsibility. But it is very unlikely that the governing body or the LEA would or, indeed, could intervene to overrule a decision legitimately and reasonably taken by the head.

The role of teaching staff

Having said that the head controls the internal organisation, it is very clear, especially in a time of teacher unrest, that this cannot be done without the co-operation and support of the staff. To take just one example, it is usually the head of department, not the head, who decides how a particular subject should be taught, or what exams should be offered. And once the individual teacher is inside the classroom, there are limits to any control over what they teach. Heads who are unhappy about a particular subject or teacher, can make suggestions, call in the LEA adviser, or suggest in-service training. They can encourage, persuade, criticise, nag, inspire, but they cannot force anyone to teach the way they want.

On the other hand, although individual teachers may appear to have a good deal of independence inside the classroom (indeed some of them might say that they could do with less freedom and more support) they often have very little say in how a school is run. Schools are still very hierarchical institutions, and although heads may claim that they consult their staff, they do not always do this very effectively. This can lead to frustration and loss of morale. It may explain why teachers sometimes appear to be unco-operative.

The role of non-teaching staff

Non-teaching staff too can exert considerable influence on the work of a school. A co-operative caretaker, and ancillary staff who are trained and care about their job can make all the difference. Yet they often report to a different superior outside the school, which can make life difficult for the head. Grounds staff may report to the Parks Department, or the cleaning and school-keeping services may be centrally organised. It is helpful to know who is responsible for whom, especially if you have cause for complaint.

The governing body

When the Articles of Government give the governing body the 'general direction' of the conduct and curriculum of the school, what does this mean in practice, given the right of the head to control internal management? By and large, as much or as little as the individual governing body wants it to mean. It can act as a rubber-stamp for decisions already taken by the head, or it can take its role more seriously.

WHO ARE THE GOVERNORS?

Until the new legislation envisaged in *Better schools* and planned for 1986 comes into force, which may take several years, many governors will continue to be political appointees. Technically these are known as LEA governors because they are appointed by the LEA. The usual custom is for the political parties to share out the LEA places on governing bodies in proportion to their representation on the local council. (There is nothing to stop the majority party taking all these places for its own nominees, and this does very occasionally happen where there is a crucial local political issue.) There must also be at least one elected teacher governor for a school of under three hundred pupils, two elected teachers for schools larger than this. In addition to the teacher governors, heads can choose whether or not to be full members of their school's governing body. Some areas also have elected non-teaching staff governors, and pupil governors. Governing bodies usually have the power to co-opt extra governors of their own choice. A few areas already have community governors, as proposed for all schools in *Better schools*. At present, these are chosen by the governing body or appointed by the LEA from people nominated by local community organisations.

In voluntary aided schools, the foundation governors, appointed according to the original trust deed establishing the school, must outnumber the other governors by two in governing bodies of eighteen or less, and by three in governing bodies of over eighteen. In voluntary controlled schools at least one-fifth of the governors must be foundation governors. This is why in voluntary aided schools, one of the parent governors is not elected by the parents, but appointed by the foundation, though in practice it may be a parent who has been chosen by the parent body.

In *Better schools* preserving the majority given to the foundation governors takes priority over increasing the representation of elected parents and teachers, so no changes are proposed for the composition of voluntary school governing bodies.

WHAT POWERS DO THE GOVERNORS HAVE?

In addition to the various powers defined in the school's Articles over such matters as appointment of staff, suspensions, premises, etc., discussed in earlier chapters of this guide, the governing body has a duty to keep under review how the school is working. The head and staff are accountable to the governing body for the way the school's aims and objectives are being achieved. This is what 'general direction' ought to mean.

It does not mean that the governors decide what should be taught or how it should be taught. It is the professional responsibility of the head and staff to prepare proposals on the aims of the school, and the policy for carrying them out and monitoring progress. These proposals are then put before the governing body for discussion and approval. Teachers sometimes resent this necessity to explain what they are doing and why they are doing it. But if professionals cannot explain and justify their course of action to the people who are affected by it, there must be serious doubts about whether the proposal is as good as it should be. The governing body performs the very useful function of testing out proposals before they are put into operation and have consequences that may not have been foreseen by their originators.

A well-informed and active governing body can also act as a channel of communication between the school and the LEA and the school and its community. It is much easier for governors living in the local community to be aware of how a school is regarded locally, and what the concerns and needs of the community are. And the governing body can also defend their school against unjust or ignorant attacks from outside.

However, the real power of the governing body does not lie in the law and regulations. It depends far more on mutual trust and respect built up between the head and staff and the governors. When you have a governing body that represents all the interests involved in a school – parents and pupils, staff, the LEA and the local community – who are used to working together on behalf of the school, that governing body has earned the right to be listened to. What is more, the LEA, the head and the staff will have to listen.

What do you do when you have a problem?

It is very upsetting for parents when a child is distressed about something that is happening at school, or when they feel that their child is not making good progress. They may be reluctant to approach the school, because they do not want to appear over-protective, and are afraid of the label 'fussy parent'. But unless you tell the school what is wrong, it is hard for the staff to do anything about it.

Who's in charge?

The first step is to find out who has the responsibility. For many minor problems, the first person to talk to will be the class teacher or form tutor. (Very often in a primary school you can speak to the teacher when you bring your child to school, but do not expect to be able to have a discussion with them on the spot. Ask when would be a good moment.) They may suggest that it would be better to speak to the deputy head, head of house or year, or the headteacher. Alternatively, write a note to the head or telephone the school office. Do not allow yourself to be put off by the school secretary, who may be over-protective of the head and staff.

If the problem is not within the school, it is even more important to talk to the person with authority. You will waste a good deal of time and energy if you present your case to the wrong people. They may listen politely, and promise to pass on your questions, but if it is not their job, or they are just carrying out a policy laid down by someone else, you are much better off finding out whose job it really is.

The simplest way to do this is to ask. Ring up the Education Offices (address in the telephone book, possibly under the name of the local authority, or the library should be able to give it to you) and ask who is in charge of school admissions, or grants or whatever. And make sure you write their name down when you track them down. If you cannot get the information this way, the *Education yearbook* may give the names of senior officers and councillors, or one of the people mentioned in the next section may be able to help.

Marshall your evidence

The second essential is to get the facts straight. Do not rely entirely on what your child tells you. Talk to other parents and children, and never make any rash statements or wild generalisations that you cannot prove. Understate rather than overstate, because any inaccuracies can be used to discredit your whole case, however justified the main part of it may be. It is a good rule always to ask for information rather than put forward criticisms. 'Jane seems to be doing very little work at home – can you tell me what the school expects children in her year to do?' is a better approach than 'Jane says she never does her homework because Miss Bloggs never bothers to mark it'.

The golden rule is never lose your temper, however provoked you may feel. Quite apart from the fact that it will not help you to say what you want to say effectively, it has the result of putting you in the wrong, however legitimate your complaint.

It helps if you can get support from other parents, and can show that you are not alone in your concern.

Who can help?

You have talked to the staff and the head, and they are unable or unwilling to help. Who else may be able to help you?

THE GOVERNING BODY

The easiest way for a parent to contact the governors is normally through the parent governors. Their names should be on display in the school, or you can ask the school office. If for some reason this does not work, the Education Offices should be able to tell you who they are. If you prefer, you can contact the chair of governors, whose name has to be published by law (see page 18).

THE LEA OFFICERS

The officers in the education department carry day-to-day responsibility, and it is always worth asking to see them to enlist their support and to find out what the rules really are. Heads are not always a hundred per cent accurate in their knowledge of the LEA regulations and policy.

COUNCIL MEMBERS

Do not forget your local councillor, who is elected to serve your interests, and may be on the Education Committee. Good councillors will have regular surgeries advertised locally, where you can bring any problems. Members of the Education Committee can do more for parents worried about schools than the local MP because they have the direct responsibility for making policy decisions about local education. A Member of Parliament may be able to put some pressure on the local council through party contacts, but does not have any real authority over local educational decisions.

LOCAL VOLUNTARY GROUPS

There are other people who may be able to give you advice or information and who would be willing to take up problems that are more general than personal. There may be a local CASE group – a branch of the Campaign for the Advancement of State Education – or a branch of the National Association of Governors and Managers, who give a lot of support to parent governors. The local library may be able to put you in touch with them, or you can write to the national secretaries of the organisations. Other voluntary organisations concerned with children may be able to help. The local Law Centre or Citizen's Advice Bureau can give impartial legal advice. These groups may have someone who can come with you to give moral and practical support in any interviews, appeals, etc.

As explained on page 157 the last resort is the Secretary of State, or, in special cases, the courts.

Local Ombudsman

If it is the way a policy has been carried out, rather than the policy itself that is at issue, the Ombudsman (commissioner for local administration) can intervene. The Ombudsman can investigate complaints about maladministration on the part of LEAs. This does not include the teaching, curriculum, internal organisation, management and discipline of a school, but it could include matters like school choice arrangements or transport to school.

Maladministration has occurred when an LEA has acted with bias, neglect, delay, or inefficiency, or when the system itself is at fault. You have to have given the school or the LEA a chance to put matters right, and you must put your complaint to a local councillor within twelve months. If nothing happens, you can then write direct to the Ombudsman yourself.

The Ombudsman can call for evidence, prepare a report stating whether or not maladministration has taken place, and if so what should be done about it. But the Ombudsman has no power to direct an LEA to put things right. If the LEA fails to act, a second report, advertising their failure, can be issued. An adverse report is very damaging to the Authority.

Running a campaign

You may find that the issue you are worried about affects other people beside yourself. A campaign is needed, and in the great majority of cases, it will not be directed towards the school, but will be designed to influence the LEA.

What makes a campaign effective?

ALLIES

The more support you can raise, the greater your chance of success.

Other parents Without the support and commitment of other parents (because you and they will have to do most of the work) you are unlikely to get far.
The head and staff You will probably find that what is worrying you has been worrying them, or some of them, for a long time. They will be only too pleased that someone is taking up the cudgels on their behalf.
The governing body You should always make an approach to the governors of all the schools involved, as it is their job to represent community interests, and you will be reaching the parent governors, who are a likely source of support.
Local voluntary groups They will have the knowledge and experience of local conditions.

LEA officers They may not be able to help you openly, but unofficially can give you all kinds of helpful hints.
Politicians Beware of identifying your campaign with any one political party. If it gets a 'political' label you have immediately alienated a large section of potential support from members of other parties.

PUBLICITY

How can you contact all these people?

Personal approaches are better than mass mailings. A few activists can spread the word, with a resulting ripple effect.
Local press. Get letters in the local press and prepare a carefully worded press release with photos if appropriate. Follow this up with 'pone calls.
Local radio. Local radio is thirsty for new items. Find out who deals with education/community affairs, and speak to them personally.
Street stalls All you need is a table in a busy shopping area, a friendly shopkeeper who does not mind you standing in front of the shop, and some leaflets and a clipboard to take names and addresses.

HOMEWORK

None of this is any good unless you have done your homework. This means hard work on research into education law and practice, statistics, local education policy (reading the committee minutes and agendas) and DES reports. If you can present the LEA with a well-written, well-argued, well-informed, rational statement of your case, you will be surprised how many doors are opened.

What you must realise is that many of those in authority care about education too, and are glad of informed support, concern and enthusiasm. If you can show that your support is broadly-based, that your object is to benefit the education of all the children in the area, not just a particular (already privileged) group, and that you have got your facts right, it is in their interest to agree with you.

And do not forget that a mass lobby of parents who are local electors has a wonderful power to concentrate the minds of councillors and candidates. The months before a local or general election are a very good time to influence local politicians.

Useful publications

This is a small selection from the many educational publications available – a browse in a bookshop near a teacher training institution, or a good reference library will demonstrate the wide choice on the market. Some of the reference books mentioned are very expensive, but they should be in a large reference library. In London, the DES library at Elizabeth House, and the ILEA Education Library in County Hall, both near Waterloo Station, are open to the public in office hours.

After school a guide to the opportunities for education and training on leaving school, by Felicity Taylor, published by Kogan Page 1984

The Auld report a report on the public enquiry into William Tyndale School, published by ILEA 1978

Better schools White paper on schools published by HMSO 1985

British qualifications comprehensive guide to all professional, technical and other qualifications, published by Kogan Page

Children and their primary schools the report of the Plowden committee on primary education, published by HMSO 1967

Choosing a school by Felicity Taylor, published by ACE 1981

Compendium of advanced courses in colleges and institutes of higher education published annually by London and Home Counties Regional Advisory Council, Tavistock House South, Tavistock Square, London WC1H 9LR; 01–388 0027

Compendium of university entrance requirements published annually by Lund Humphries

COPE – compendium of post-school education for children with disabilities, by Chas Lillystone and Liz Summerson, available from National Bureau for Handicapped Students

Directory of grant-making trusts published by Charities Aid Foundation.

Education for all, the report of the Swann committee of enquiry into the education of ethnic minorities, published by HMSO 1985

Educational opportunities for all? the Fish report on provision for special educational needs in the ILEA, published by ILEA 1985

Education yearbook comprehensive guide to LEAs and educational facilities, published by Longman 1986

The effective school governor by Joan Sallis, published by ACE 1980

Equal opportunities and the school governor published by the Equal Opportunities Commission 1985, free

Fifteen thousand hours a report of a research project on secondary schools and their effects on children, by Rutter, Maughan, Mortimore and Ouston, published by Open Books 1979

Fit for the future the Court report on child health services, published by HMSO 1976

Improving primary schools the Thomas report on primary education in the ILEA, published by the ILEA 1984

Improving secondary schools the Hargreaves report on secondary education in the ILEA, published by the ILEA 1984

The law of education, looseleaf, constantly updated guide to education law, circulars and memoranda, published by Butterworths

A new partnership for our schools, the Taylor report on school government published by HMSO 1976

Out in the open? the school records debate, by Lucy Hodges, published by Writers and Readers Co-operative 1981

Records of achievement at 16 by Tyrrell Burgess and Elizabeth Adams, published by Nelson/NFER 1985

School governors' guide with useful glossary of educational jargon, by Barbara Bullivant, published by Home and School Council 1980

School governor's handbook and training guide by Anne Sofer and Tyrrell Burgess, published by Kogan Page, second edition 1986

Special educational needs the report of the Warnock committee on special education, published by HMSO 1978

Special education handbook, by Peter Newell, published by ACE, second edition 1985

Teaching quality White paper on teacher education, published by HMSO 1983

UCCA handbook, how to apply for admission to university, published annually by UCCA, free

Vandalism in schools, by Judith Stone and Felicity Taylor, published by Save the Children, 1977

Where to look things up, A–Z sources on educational topics, by Elizabeth Wallis, published by ACE

Your choice series on how to choose option subjects at different ages, published by CRAC

Educational press

ACE bulletin on educational issues for parents and others, ten issues a year on subscription only

Education weekly journal for education administrators, but much useful information for parents and governors, published by Longman, Fridays

Education Guardian Tuesday's edition of the *Guardian* carries a large education section of general interest

Times educational supplement weekly newspaper for teachers, with all the latest news and views, Fridays

Useful addresses

Advisory Centre for Education (ACE)
18 Victoria Park Square, London E2 9PB; 01-980 4596.

British Psychological Society St Andrew's House, 48 Princess Road East, Leicester LE1 7DR; 0533 549568

Campaign for the Advancement of State Education (CASE) National Secretary, 4 Hill Road, Carshalton Beeches, Surrey; 01-669 5929

Careers and Occupational Information Centre (COIC)
Moorfoot, Sheffield S1 4PQ; 0742 753275

Careers Research and Advisory Centre (CRAC) Hobson's Press (Cambridge) Ltd, Bateman Street, Cambridge CB2 1LZ; 0223 354551

Centre for Studies in Integration in Education
16 Fitzroy Square London W1P 5HQ; 01-387 9571

Chartered Institute of Public Finance and Accountancy (CIPFA)
3 Robert Street, London WC2; 01-930 3456

Children's Legal Centre 20 Compton Terrace, London N1 2UN; 01-359 9392.

Commission for Racial Equality Elliot House, Allington Street, London SW1E 5EH; 01-828 7022

Conference for Independent Further Education (CIFE)
PO Box 80, Guildford, Surrey GU1 2NL; 0483 69680

Department of Education and Science (DES) Elizabeth House, York Road, London SE1 7PH; 01-934 9000. DES Publications Despatch Centre, Honeypot Lane, Canons Park, Stanmore HA7 1AZ; 01-952 2366

Educational Counselling and Credit Transfer Information Service (ECCTIS) PO Box 88, Sherwood Drive, Bletchley MK3 6DL; 0908 71131

Educational Publishers Council 19 Bedford Square, London WC1B 3HJ; 01-580 6321

Education Otherwise 25 Common Lane, Hemmingford Abbots, Cambridgeshire TE18 9AN; 0480 63131

Equal Opportunities Commission (EOC) Overseas House, Quay St, Manchester M3 3HN; 061-833 9244.
Higher Education Information Service Middlesex Polytechnic, Chase Side, London N14 5PN; 01-886 6599
Independent Schools Information Service (ISIS) 56 Buckingham Gate, London SW1G 6AH; 01-630 8793
National Association of Governors and Managers (NAGM) National Secretary, 81 Rustlings Road, Sheffield S11 7AB; 0742 662467. NAGM Regional Training Programme, 10 Brookfield Park, London NW5 1ER; 01-485 4258.
National Bureau for Handicapped Students 40 Brunswick Square, London WC1N 1AZ; 01-278 3450
National Confederation of Parent Teacher Associations (NCPTA) 43 Stonebridge Road, Northfleet, Gravesend, Kent; 0474 60618
National Union of Students 461 Holloway Road, London N7 6LJ; 01-272 8900
Ombudsmen
Commissioner for local administration in England, 21 Queen Anne's Gate, London SW1H 9BU; 01-722 5622
Commissioner for local administration in Wales, Derwen House, Court Road, Bridgend, Mid Glamorgan CF31 1BN; 0656 61325
Commissioner for local administration in Scotland, 5 Shandwick Place, Edinburgh EH2 4RG; 031-229 4472
Playboard Head Office, Britannia House, 50 Great Charles Street, Queensway, Birmingham B3 2LP; 021-233 3399
Polyscan North Staffordshire Polytechnic, Blackheath Lane, Stafford; 0785 53511.
Pre-school Playgroups Association Alford House, Aveline Street, London SE11 5DH; 01-582 8871
Release (advice about drugs etc) 1 Elgin Avenue, London W9; 01-289 1123; 24hr emergency service 01–603 8654
Universities Central Council on Admissions (UCCA) PO Box 28, Cheltenham, Glos GL50 1HY
Voluntary Council for Handicapped Children 8 Wakley Street, London EC1V 7QE; 01-278 9441

Index